MULTIMIND

By Robert Ornstein

On the Experience of Time

On the Psychology of Meditation
(with C. Naranjo)

The Psychology of Consciousness
(first and second editions)

The Nature of Human Consciousness

Symposium on Consciousness

Common Knowledge

The Mind Field

The Amazing Brain
(with R. Thompson and D. Macaulay)

Psychology: The Study of Human Experience
(an introductory text)

The Psychology of Consciousness
(the classic study completely revised and updated)

Multimind

ROBERT ORNSTEIN

MULTIMIND

ANCHOR BOOKS
DOUBLEDAY
NEW YORK LONDON TORONTO SYDNEY AUCKLAND

AN ANCHOR BOOK

PUBLISHED BY DOUBLEDAY

a division of Bantam Doubleday Dell Publishing Group, Inc.

666 Fifth Avenue, New York, New York 10103

ANCHOR BOOKS, DOUBLEDAY, and the portrayal of an anchor
are trademarks of Doubleday, a division of Bantam Doubleday
Dell Publishing Group, Inc.

The author is grateful for permission to use material from the following sources:
The Magic Monastery by Idries Shah. Published by Octagon Press, London, 1972.
The Minds of Billy Milligan by Daniel Keyes. Copyright © 1981 by Daniel Keyes and
William S. Milligan. Reprinted by permission of Random House, Inc., and Bantam
Books, Inc. All rights reserved.
Influence by Robert B. Cialdini. Published by Scott, Foresman and Company, Glenview,
Ill., 1984.
The Quiet Furies: Man and Disorder by Elton B. McNeil. Copyright © 1967. Reprinted by
permission of Prentice-Hall, Inc., Englewood Cliffs, N.J.
The figures on pages 38, 42, and 117 are reprinted from *Psychology: The Study of
Human Experience* by Robert Ornstein, published by Harcourt Brace Jovanovich, Inc.,
1985. The figure on page 42 originally appeared in *Sensory Communication* by Walter A.
Rosenblith, published by MIT Press. The figure on page 117 originally appeared in
Cognitive Psychology (vol. 11, 1979), published by Academic Press.

This book was originally published in hardcover by
Houghton Mifflin Company in 1986. The Anchor Books edition
is published by arrangement with the author.

Library of Congress Cataloging-in-Publication Data
Ornstein, Robert E. (Robert Evan), 1942–
Multimind / Robert Ornstein. — 1st Anchor books ed.
p.   cm.
Originally published: Boston : Houghton, Mifflin, 1986.
Bibliography: p.
ISBN 0-385-26446-1
1. Intellect.   2. Brain.   I. Title
BF431.068   1989   89-34045
150—dc20   CIP

*For Sally
and for
each and every one
of her minds.
May they all meet
one day.*

CONTENTS

PART I

MIND ON MIND

Nasrudin went into a bank with a cheque to cash.
"Can you identify yourself?" asked the clerk.
Nasrudin took out a mirror and peered into it.
"Yes, that's me all right," he said.
— Idries Shah, *The Subtleties
of the Inimitable Mulla Nasrudin*

The story is one of the "subtleties" of Nasrudin. But
Idries Shah's work, while it would be notable well enough
for selecting and collecting tales which anchor us on
angles of our personality, goes much further. Shah,
miraculously, has done what I would have once believed
to be completely impossible; he has refreshed and
revolutionized the Western idea and ideal of the mind.

His stories, about Nasrudin and others, drawn from
ancient Middle Eastern and current Western traditions,
anticipate modern brain and cognitive science, in some
cases by a millennium! But it is not precedence which
leads me to extract and entreat you to read his books.
No. It is that the characters in Shah's stories, taken
alone and taken together, mirror the multiple selves
inside *ourself* and reflect them to us. His work has
guided me among many, to look at the components of
our mind, and hold them up, separately, so that we can
see that each of us is a *variety* of people, not one alone.

CHAPTER ONE

Introduction: Many Diverse Points on the Many Diverse Problems of Understanding the Mind

IT WAS Marilyn Monroe who first got me thinking about the puzzling nature of the mind.

Of course, she stimulated my first thoughts about many things, but something happened after her death that stuck in my mind. Her suicide was a shock to me and to many others, but that was not so puzzling.

For the next few months, I kept reading about many other suicides, and all of it began to bother me. Why were so many people killing themselves after Marilyn Monroe did so? It wasn't that people were grieving that much: many of the suicides had hardly heard of her. But the overall suicide rate in the USA went up by 12 percent after Marilyn's suicide; then it went down again.

I forgot about Marilyn and her suicide for many years. Then the comedian Freddie Prinze killed himself and the same thing happened. The suicide rate shot up by 8 percent for a while.

This and many other apparently puzzling things happen to us because of the way our mind is segmented.

Part of the approach of this book stems from my conviction that, while one can learn much about the mind from reading the great philosophers and psychologists, there is much to discover by observing other people and considering many daily events.

You walk along Fifty-seventh Street, quietly minding your own business. A balloon man leaps in front of you and says, "A free balloon if you smile." You can't resist. You smile. You get a free balloon. And, of course, you buy something from him, although buying a balloon was hardly the top thing on your mind. However, the balloon man's maneuver helped make it so.

In a college town in the Midwest, a young man named Billy Milligan was arrested for raping a woman. The psychologist interviewing him asked for his social security number.

> He shrugged, "I don't know."
> The psychologist read his number to him.
> . . . "That's not my number, it must be Billy's."
> . . . "Well, aren't you Billy?"
> "I'm David."
> "Well, where's Billy?"
> "He's asleep."
> "Asleep where?"
> He pointed to his chest. "In here. He's asleep."
> . . . "I have to talk to Billy."
> "Well, Arthur won't let you. Billy's asleep. Arthur won't wake him up, 'cause if he does, Billy'll kill himself."

One might dismiss all these different "people" inside as a criminal's elaborate ruse to avoid conviction, but the Ohio authorities finally did not. Although "Billy Milligan" committed the crime, it was judged that another "person" inside him was responsible and that Billy as a whole could not be punished for the crime of one of his parts. A course of treatment to attempt to fuse the different personalities was prescribed and was successful.

A friend says to you: "My first marriage broke up because my wife had different political opinions than I. My second wife shared my opinions, but we constantly fought over how to bring up the children. My third wife and I agree on everything like that, and we get along well, but I can't understand so much about her: she doesn't think it is wrong to pad her expense account at work, and she cheats on her income tax. When do I find someone who is perfect for me?"

You go out to a restaurant for the first time. Your waiter tells you not to order the steak Diane, at $23.95, but to have the veal, at $19.95, "because it's fresh." You think he's great and buy a very expensive wine on his recommendation as well as an extra salad for everyone. Since he is in the tip business, he makes out well and you love him and return the following week for more of his recommendations.

A poor child is never taught to read by his mother, nor is he taught about the life of Abraham Lincoln. In a one-hour paper and pencil test, he cannot identify Lincoln or any of his achievements. He thus does very badly on his one general intelligence test and is assigned to a "slow" track in school because his IQ is low. Many of his mathematical talents then go to waste.

A recent cover of *People* headlines:

Devout Buddhist
$5,000 an hour shopper

Mother of four
World class vamp

And how many people are being described? Tina Turner.

Here are more headline stories, all of these from a few months in early 1985.

A family named Walker is accused of selling secrets to the Russians. After the spy scandal breaks, the U.S. Secretary of Defense says that we really must cut some of the five million people who have security clearance. A member of the Senate is interviewed on television and says that it is easier to get security clearance than it is to get an American Express card. Did no one notice this before the scandal?

A chemical leak in a Union Carbide plant in Bhopal, India, exposes hundreds of thousands of people to toxic fumes and causes severe damage to the health of at least twenty thousand. Soon after, hundreds of stories appear in the press announcing the threat to *our* safety of all the improperly stored chemicals in the United States, describing the generally dangerous and defective safety and storage procedures in many chemical and industrial plants.

The famous movie star Rock Hudson reveals that he has AIDS. Funds for research are increased dramatically only a few days later. An announcer on *ABC News* said at the time that "AIDS has received more attention in the few weeks after Rock Hudson's announcement than in the previous four years." Another former movie star gets colon cancer; the phone at the American Cancer Society rings off the hook. Because of the widespread publicity, thousands of people may well detect this form of cancer early because they are stimulated to have checkups.

Why do we need shocks and vivid disasters to goad us into action? Why does an event like the suicide of a famous movie star have such influence over the lives and deaths of many? Why do we assume so much about other people only to be disappointed? Why do we judge and test others so harshly? We don't know ourselves well enough, I think.

It has been about a hundred years since the beginnings of modern psychology and fifty or so years since the development of modern brain science. It is about time we bring together the evidence: the way we understand ourselves and the way we understand others is incomplete and misleading.

At the core of many of our controversies—some intellectual, some philosophical, some personal—is an oversimplified understanding of the nature of our mind. We may ask: Should I act on my emotions or on what I think? Are we rational or does an "unconscious" set our agenda? Are our mental faculties the product of experiences or of learning? Is she conscientious or lazy, is he honorable or sometimes dishonest? The answers to these and to many other supposed either/or controversies is "both."

We often hate ourselves for not behaving as we "should": Why did I get so nervous? Why did I blush when he said that? Why did I buy that expensive pool table when I don't have much money? We are bothered a lot by our behavior: otherwise, why would our face and body posture betray a lie?

It is an odd situation if you consider it: Why are some of the things we do so unacceptable to ourselves? It is because we are not single-minded: *the part of ourself that is often judging is independent from the part that is behaving.*

There is a new view arising about the nature of the brain and the mind:

Stuck side by side, inside the skin, inside the skull, are several special purpose, separate, and specific small minds.

The particular collection of talents, abilities, and capacities that each person possesses depends partly on birth and partly on experience. Our illusion is that each of us is somehow unified, with a single coherent purpose and action. Others present a smooth, seemingly consistent and unified surface as well. But it *is* an illusion, as we are hidden from ourselves, just as the skin covers a lot of different organs that are only visible once the covering has been lifted.

Similarly, the brain case screens from our view the diversity of the human brain. It has taken the evidence of the past few decades to discern the different separate mental structures that lie, almost hidden, deep within the homogeneous mass of the brain. It has taken us a long time to break the covering of the different minds within, but as a result our view of our own nature is in for a radical change.

"I am large, there is a multitude within," wrote Whitman.

We have inescapable and built-in deceptions and illusions about ourselves. These illusions have caused many of our historically important philosophers and psychologists to overemphasize a single human ability as representative of the entire mind.

There is a fairly standard process of human discovery that we go through when we try to understand anything new. The explorers' first maps of exotic places like Africa showed a simple, undifferentiated continent. Only later, with much more research, did the complexity of the terrain become clear. An appreciation of the complexity and subtlety of painting, music, food, and ideas follows the same pattern.

We have gone through the same process in understanding the nature of the human mind. Our view of ourselves is limited by the very structures of the mind itself. We do not have, really, any privileged access to understanding ourselves; in fact, our own introspection is often just an illusion.

We are not a single person.

We are many.

The long progression in our self-understanding has been from a simple and usually "intellectual" view to the view that the mind is a mixed structure, for it contains a complex set of "talents," "modules," and "policies" within. (These terms are unfamiliar, I know, but they will be discussed at length.) All of these general components of the mind can act independently of each other, they may well have different priorities.

The discovery of increased complexity and differentiation has occurred in many different areas of research that touch upon this book: in the study of brain function and localization; in the conceptions of the nature of intelligence; in personality testing; and in the theories of the general characteristics of the mind. We shall have something to say about each aspect.

It should not be surprising that we possess such a simplified understanding of ourselves because the mind operates to simplify: it reduces the complexity of the outside world to standard items easy to act on. For example: circles the shape of slivers still signify round plates; cars that look like toys are still treated as real but distant; a friend's voice over the phone summons up the rest of the person—the opinions, ideas, likely judgments. As the brain and skin cover and hide discrepancy and conflict within, so our simplified and selected perceptions hide others' and our real complexity and richness.

There have been many important and certainly long-lasting arguments about the nature of human knowledge. These are the ones we have grown up with and almost absorbed through our pores in school. Perhaps the most important argument for the last two millennia has been the one between the "rationalists," from Descartes on, and the "empiricists," from Aristotle through Locke and behaviorism. It concerns the degree to which we have innate knowledge of the world, abilities such as the understanding of language without special learning. More and more modern evidence makes it clear that we are given a large innate endowment of faculties with which we perceive and understand the world.

But the modern evidence shows us more. This important argument is not so much out of date but pertains to only a small portion of the mind, one that can be analyzed, put in words, on computers, in logical programs, and one that is suitable for and similar to academic thought.

Most of us have grown up assuming that we are the products of our environment and that anyone can be trained to learn almost anything. A mind trained to reason and analyze can yield limitless accomplishments.

While many important thinkers from Plato onward had a different perspective, the main influence on our thinking, society, and education stems from Locke and Hume, developing a line of thought from Aristotle. Logic and intellection are the components of mind, and knowledge comes from experience. The Western intellectual tradition has in the past few thousand years developed this initial program about as far as it will go.

If Western philosophy is, as someone once said, a set of footnotes to the Greeks, then modern brain and psychological science has ushered in a new chapter.

It is time for a new perspective.

A major part of the twentieth-century challenge to this simple intellectual view has come from a view that is often opposed to the intellectual tradition. It is called the analytic tradition, referring to the psychoanalytic work stemming from Sigmund Freud and his critics and followers.

Both traditions have existed side by side for almost a century now, with neither making any real inroads into the other. Freud and his followers posited a complex structure to the mind in which the conscious, rational part was likened to the tip of an iceberg. Underneath was the repository of wishes, plans, and desires that were not accessible to the rational conscious. Thus people would make slips of the tongue, make motivated mistakes, and behave irrationally but in a way that would fulfill unconscious needs and desires.

There has been a tension and a lack of communication between these two traditions: the pure intellectuals of the Western intellectual tradition and those challenging the single-minded view from outside, for whom Freud and his followers have provided an important alternative.

Each of these great traditions is really quite primitive. They are most often limited to an extreme emphasis upon one way of looking at the mind, and they most often confuse the phenomena that they emphasize with the whole. For one group, the emphasis is on human reason and learning and the possibility of progress through intellection. For the other, the focus is largely on many basic instinctual drives and the many levels of unconscious desire. These are thought to make the mind unstable; in Freud's pessimistic view, we are doomed to continuous conflict since we possess such an irrational system. We can, from a more modern perspective, combine these insights in a more complete picture.

This book is about why we have the kind of mental system we do and how it got to be that way, what it is good for, and how it has reached a breaking point in the modern world, a world for which it was not made. The book is also about how it is almost inevitable that we so grossly misunderstand ourselves and each other.

The first section contains a general sketch of the operations of our mental system. The second reviews the physiological and evolutionary evidence that we have a brain and nervous system best described as multiple, "designed" to carry out many different programs at the same time. These include different talents, like the ability to talk and to calculate.

The third part concerns current evidence of cognitive psychology, the psychology of consciousness, perception, memory, and thinking. It shows that human consciousness is by necessity extremely limited and therefore *only a small portion of the mind operates on the main stage at once.* Thus our minds are easily altered, our judgments shifted from moment to moment, by the way in which problems are framed and by which portion of the mind is operating at a given instant.

The fourth section considers some of the problems: the tragedy of intelligence testing; the difficulty of attaining a complete and satisfying understanding of another person; and the breakups of the mind that reveal the subpersonalities below.

The last chapter considers a point that many will wish answered: Who is doing the controlling, if anybody? It also discusses how a greater measure of self-understanding and control might be attained by observing one's own inconsistencies and shifts of mood. I would not say this book builds to a conclusion, but I hope that it will open a few doors and make you think about problems, personal and intellectual, that might now be tackled.

Together with the reviews of evidence on mind and brain, intelligence and personality, I wish to present a new perspective on the human mind, one that encompasses the philosophical arguments, the challenges from Freud and from the discoveries of evolution, the new evidence from brain sciences and cognition, the problems of intelligence and personality and multiple personality. I hope this viewpoint will allow many who now see only myriad opposing and conflicting small and useless minor theories to understand that many of the conflicts have been caused by looking at the mind as if it had only one aspect, the aspect that is most highly prized in schools.

Such a concentration on verbal talents and rational sequential analysis has led to a spectacular series of triumphs in our society. We can bounce a signal off the moon, make wafers in space the size of a micron, create weapons in one submarine that have the firepower of all of World War II. But our other talents are not educated or developed along with the reasoning ones.

Our ability to produce has far outstripped our ability to judge what we are doing. We are close to destroying the earth in a few moments with bombs or, in a few years, with the increasing burden of people. We don't know how to feed, clothe, and develop the people we have. We are in a race with ourselves, inside our own minds.

But back to Descartes for a moment.

CHAPTER TWO

The Mind *Wheels*

Cogito: ergo sum.
— Descartes

THERE IS A DOMINANT Greek myth, derived from Aristotle, that remains with us: we are thinkers first, and thinkers most.

We return to René Descartes' famous assertion "I think, therefore I am" because it has always seemed to be the clearest single statement of the idea that we, the entire human being, exist only in our thinking abilities. (I do not in any way, however, mean to belittle Descartes' great contributions to our understanding of ourselves. Although one could argue it, his analysis was one of the major turning points that led to the modern understanding of the mind and brain.)

Descartes was quite unimpressed with the two millennia of philosophy that preceded him, finding it lacking in any idea of the mechanisms of the mind. While he may have overreacted, his violent rejection led him to a radical solution. In attempting to understand the basic nature of the mind, Descartes discarded most of what was then known and thought.

His method was hermetic. He repaired to a farm in Bavaria and systematically cast doubt on every philosophical doctrine from the Greeks onward, leaving himself with only his doubts themselves and the basic intuitions of mathematics. "I *doubt*, therefore" might have been a better slogan.

Descartes then came to the realization that much human knowledge was innate; it existed within the structure of the brain and nervous system. He then proposed that there exists an innate set of abilities through which the mind directs the automaton of a body. He even proposed a physical location for this interaction, the *pineal* of the brain, for it is the one organ of the brain whose structure is single rather than dual. He was most important because he set the modern era of the study of mind-brain relations in motion:

> What must be the fabric of the nerves and muscles of the human body in order that the animal spirits therein should have the power to move the members . . . what changes are necessary in the brain to cause wakefulness, sleep and dream; how light, sounds, smells, tastes, and all other qualities pertaining to external objects are able to imprint on it various ideas by the intervention of the senses.

Descartes also developed the modern understanding that somehow the mind must possess an internal representation of external reality. Thus we construct a kind of model inside the head which is used by the person to operate the world, just as a globe is a model of the real world. Our globes are probably not accurate, but they are good enough to tell us whether Scotland is generally north or south of Wales.

Both these ideas—that there are specific mind and brain relationships and that the mind creates a representation of the world—were important and influential contributions. Descartes also brought up much of the modern questioning on the relationship of mind and brain in a more detailed way than had been done before. Here we will follow a rather simple and naive position on this problem: that the mind in some way depends on the specific brain structures but is not identical to them.

But Descartes' "mind," whether it had innate ideas or whether (as was challenged) it learned entirely from experiences, was later reduced to simplicity by the philosophers who have had such influence on the modern mind. The mind has been reduced by many in our intellectual tradition to a single and ultimately reasonable entity, one that would become more and more understandable by the intellect. This view has influenced most of us, whether or not we are professional philosophers or academics or educators. We now know it to be in large part incomplete and too simple.

The idea that we have one rational mind seriously undersells our diverse abilities. It oversells our consistency, and it emphasizes the very small, rational islands in the mind at the expense of the vast archipelago of talents, opportunities, and abilities surrounding them.

We often assume that our own mind is a reasonable and stable, somewhat solid device. It is not. It moves, it careens from one idea to another, and it is surprisingly inconsistent and unstable. But we have a difficult time seeing it.

I often wondered how this came to be, how scientists and philosophers for so long ignored the obvious evidence. Babies clearly follow an innate program of maturation and clearly have diverse mental abilities from birth; people have quite different talents. And many people are quite inconsistent and act very differently even at different times of the day. How could we ignore the evidence that an emergency or strong emotions like joy and disgust can completely alter the priorities and the contents of our minds?

I had assumed this lack of understanding to be an ordinary scientific problem. Did I miss something in the behaviorists' analysis? Was the evidence for such inconsistency and individuality really so poor?

It was not a question of a flaw in the methods of science. It was much simpler, and therefore more difficult for me to see, as I was teaching and working in the academic world. Scientists, like every other professional group, are selected on their particular personal abilities. This selection process has unintended effects: abilities needed for one discipline tend to influence the judgment of those in it. Academics judge others on the basis of how their academic qualities are developed. Lawyers judge people on their "lawyerly" qualities; swimmers look at the musculature and the smoothness of movements. It is hard to imagine what dancing might be if it were choreographed by lawyers!

It is a simple-minded mistake that all of us make: we assume others are like us and we judge people on our own set of criteria. People who gravitate to responsible academic positions in education and psychology have proven skills in logic, rationality, and verbal ability. It is a simple extension, for those professorially inclined, to assume that the average human mind is something like the one they idealize in their professional life. It is a wonderful structure, unimpaired by unruly emotion, never derailed by drunkenness, pain, or the weather.

The ideal mind in this view is intellectual; it contains logic and verbal abilities and is able to be educated by formal instruction. Its contents should be assessed in the same neat and formal way. This is what education has been about in our society. "Education" as a word comes from the Greeks: it refers to the "calling out" of innate verbal and mathematical skills.

With this conception of the mind as the model, it was

easy for the early educators and psychologists to make many other mistakes. Intelligence slowly became defined as those logical operations that predicted success in school and that were easy to measure in a short time using simple verbal paper and pencil tests. So, since we all go through a similar education, our idea of a fine mind is something absorbed, consciously or not, from our teachers, our professors, and from our textbooks: the mind is an organ, finely honed on argument, reason, logic, and mathematics. When we say that someone has a fine mind, we really mean that someone has a fine mouth — or, at least, a fine pen.

The assumption is that the mind was only made for thinking and reasoning. Many psychologists have tried to systematize the rules of cognition and of the operation of the brain, rules whose discovery will enable us to understand this thinking machine. Computers are used to simulate the intelligent operations of the mind; major conferences are called of eminent "cognitive scientists" to discuss arguments about how "rational" we are and how we can become more so.

I have had a chance to observe this phenomenon at first hand, sometimes with comical results. I live in Silicon Valley and the excitement of computers is in the air. In the cafés and even at the vegetable stands I hear discussions about whether there will be a gigabit chip and how soon (a gigabit is a billion bits of information, or, in current terms, 125 megabytes) and, of course, what kinds of interesting machines we have. And I am constantly invited to see a new computer development — the voice operation of word processors, prosthetic devices, new robots. I'm usually delighted.

But one day a group of friends asked me to see their new, million-dollar computer simulation of a 24-year-old neurotic female. Joking aside — does the world really need such a machine at taxpayers' expense? — I wondered whether there was any reason to go, but I went.

Questions were asked of the machine, which answered on the teleprinter. These computer people were trying to carry out Turing's Test: if you cannot tell the difference between a person and a machine, the simulation is successful. The machine typed answers to questions just as any other neurotic typist would, I guess. Then they asked us skeptics in the audience to try to determine whether the machine was really the neurotic typist or just a well-programmed computer.

When I typed in "Can you come in here and give me a kiss?" they all felt I was not playing the game fairly. I thought for a second that I was in *Gulliver's Travels*. These people were the victims of their own small-mindedness in their own small circle, in which only a small set of problems are allowed to be answered. One of them said, almost as a smug joke, "After all, a computer doesn't have a body, Bob!"

That's right! It's just too bad for the current computer simulation vogue that the mind *does* have a body to run and that it is profoundly influenced by the state of that body. It responds to body chemistry, to internal emergencies and discrepancies, to the changes in weather; it is no "information-processing" machine, not information processing as computerlanders know it. We cannot have a complete understanding let alone simulation of the mind that ignores the bodily needs, ignores the way we evolved and are built on an ancient floor plan, ignores that we are animals who must survive first.

These computer simulation scientists and the many other descendants of Aristotle suffer from a condition that has come to be known as *academiomemesis*. It is the disorder that makes one think that a human being is really like a small academic. In this condition, a living human being is thus usually thought to consist of the pure verbal and logical processes. A victim of this disorder thus gives little attention to many other dimensions of the person—feelings, personal concerns, bodily needs, the ability to sing and dance, or the ability to get along with many different kinds of people. But funny as it may seem, this limited view is no joke. It is the dominant view of what is known as "the Western intellectual tradition," a view that might be remembered by its acronym, *TWIT*.

The assumption is that the mind is the sum of the TWIT abilities: to discuss, debate, delineate, and dismiss. It assumes that people are always trying, usually rationally, to determine what is happening to them, and in a way that allows them to discuss it with others. Jean Piaget and Jerome Bruner, to take two examples, analyze a child's development as a progression of increasing thought and inference. But most of us, for most of our lives, do not try to determine the causes of things. Rather, most of the time we try to get by; to eat, sleep, and, of course, to reproduce. In other words, we are mainly concerned with surviving, getting along in a complex and changing world, in short, with adapting rather than with inference.

It is illusory to think that a person has one mind, good or bad. There is no single mind but many; we are a coalition, not a single person. The unity we experience—it is the same me that loves as reasons; it is the same me that is the father as the son; it is the same me who goes to work and plays games—is simply an illusion. It is a needed but fundamental illusion about ourselves and others because we are not consistent. We are not coherent. We do not always decide things reasonably. We are unaware of how we decide and even "who" is deciding for us.

We are unaware of the nature of our divided and diverse mental system. In fact, we have lots of minds and they are specialized to handle different chores. I am sure that this is as unsettling to many people as Freud's ideas were a century ago. But the multimind idea does not postulate that we are completely out of control, only that we do not know often enough what is in our mind or, rather, which portion of the mind is operating at any one time.

There are different kinds of memories. Some people are good at learning by rote; some have a good memory for names, some for people, some for places; some people remember conversations; others forget errands and chores; some can retrieve the right bit of information at the right time. These are all fairly separate mental abilities, and different people have their own combination of them.

There are multiple talents: spatial, verbal, intuitive, feeling, mathematical, personal, bodily, and more. Different groups of people, different segments of a society, and different cultures may have very different emphases on these skills. There exist, too, the harrowing case of multiple personalities and the diversity revealed by the knife of the surgeon or the blow to the head, jarring loose a piece of the mind.

The TWIT view leads into areas that are perhaps less productive than others. Its bias is to look to small, elegant solutions and to "optimal" ways in which the nervous system might function. But elegance and grace came, for the most part, long after the nervous system was designed. What most animals need is not elegance but adequacy, the ability to get along well enough in their environment and no better. While Dr. Pangloss may have a point sometimes, this is not the best of all possible worlds and we are not the best of all possible organisms.

Many scientists are now busy at work on a new kind of mental catalogue, one that tries to make a neat list of the many static and separate abilities, each in its own domain:

the seven kinds of memory; the six, seven, or eight kinds of intelligence and emotions; and the very many styles of thinking. They act like emperors dividing a new territory. They are producing a more complex, more detailed, but still static model of the mind.

It does not happen like that.

The mind *wheels*.

It *wheels* from condition to condition, from emergency to quiescence, from happiness to concern. As it wheels among different states, it selects the various components of the mind which operate in that state. I'll stretch "the mind *wheels*" to include this selection process: it "wheels in" segments of the mind which are designed for quite limited and specific purposes, such as a comparison program for judging weight or an innate emotional routine for acting on anger. But the mind is not neat: sometimes it does not wheel these "small minds" out fast enough, so misjudgments are made. When you come home angry because your raise was rejected, you will be more likely to find fault with your spouse's cooking, as that small mind containing the feeling reactions has not yet been "wheeled out."

Some of the small minds that get wheeled in are the result of the many diverse centers of control of the brain. These centers have developed over millions of years to regulate the body, to guard against danger, and generally to organize and plan effort. The separate mental components have different priorities and are often at cross purposes, with each other and with our life today, but they do exist and, more soberly, "they" are us. It would be a good idea, I think, if we could come to see the primitive bases of many of our judgments and decisions so that we might try to do something about them.

Our problem as individuals is that most often we act

unconsciously and automatically, thus we do not often know which one of the multiple "small minds" is operating at any time. And often we do not select the appropriate "small minds" at the right time.

We have a simple-minded view of other people as well because of the way our mental system operates. It is inevitable — and tragic — that we try to type others with a single number for intelligence or a single adjective, like "nice" or "aggressive," as if people could be reduced to one characteristic. Then we are stunned when the person so reduced behaves differently than he "should"!

The problem for scientists is to understand this diverse and complex human mental system without trying too quickly to come up with another neat model for it — even a neat model with 6 or 37 or 120 factors of mind, all nicely arranged. We were built without a neat and well-organized plan (and probably would have been rejected by computer simulation scientists), built with differing priorities over many eras. Each one of us is a crowd of people, and in this book I hope to open the way to looking at the composition and competition of that internal crowd.

CHAPTER THREE

The Mental Operating System: Its Policies and Procedures

INSTEAD OF A SINGLE, intellectual entity that can judge many different kinds of events equably, the mind is diverse and complex. It contains a changeable conglomeration of different kinds of "small minds"—fixed reactions, talents, flexible thinking—and these different entities are temporarily employed—"wheeled into consciousness"—and then usually discarded, returned to their place, after use.

One system describes these different factions of the mind. I think the best name for it is the *mental operating system*, MOS in shorthand. It is not an omnipotent controller but a semiorganized central factor in the mind, and it is often overridden by lower forces in the mind.

This is quite a different position from the single-mind view, but it may help us understand why we misjudge people so often; why we are so inconsistent; why moods, once they occur, color other thoughts, then pass away; why some people seem "possessed" for longer or shorter periods; why others can think some thoughts only when drunk, angry, elated, or depressed.

It is not a neat or even an accurate system, this mental "system" of ours. And only in the narrowest dreams of

academics could it be believed to be predominantly or even
possibly rational. The underpinnings of mind were in existence for millennia before rationality was invented.

The mental system of human beings and other animals
allows us (more probably, it allowed our close ancestors)
to simplify and to make sense out of an enormous amount
of shifting and chaotic external and internal information
and to adapt to the world sufficiently well to survive. It
doesn't have to be perfect, perfect to the academic standards
of philosophers and cognitive scientists.

I think the MOS can be best encapsulated as a system
evolved *to possess extreme sensitivity to recent information*. It
simplifies the mass of information reaching us from the
internal and external worlds by registering only sharp
changes in the information reaching it. So it can organize
lots of information into simple meaningful snippets that
allow us to act quickly.

In less jargon-laden terms, some important MOS habits
and procedures that organize, direct, and guide much of
the mind's activities are these:

1. *What have you done for me lately?*
We are extremely sensitive to recent information; emotional upsets like bad feelings last for a while, then are
forgiven. Terrible disasters like an air crash force attention on airliners for a while; all sorts of reforms are ini-
tiated and then the spotlight goes away.
2. *Don't call me unless anything new and exciting happens.*
We are interested only in "the news," the sudden appearance of something unknown. Unexpected or extraordinary events seem to have fast access to consciousness,
while an unchanging background noise, a constant weight,
or a chronic problem soon gets shunted into the background. It is easy to raise money for emergencies, like the

few victims of a well-publicized disaster; it is much more
difficult to raise money for the many victims of continuous
malnutrition. We respond quickly to scarcity and danger.

Gradual changes in the world go unnoted while sharp
changes are immediately seized on by the mind. Gasoline
prices increased in the 1970s from about 30 cents per gal-
lon to about 95 cents with little decrease in consumption.
When prices went over $1.00 there was a sharp decrease
in consumption, for we had been awakened somehow by
the change. This happens too in the simple sensory reg-
istration of information: a sudden loud noise is commanding, a continual low din as in a factory next door is
well (probably too well) tolerated.

3. The famous psychological theorist and comedian Henny
Youngman was asked: "How do you like your wife?" *"Compared to what?"* he responded.

Youngman's answer points to two phenomena: we constantly judge by comparison, and our judgment of any
item depends upon what we are comparing it to at that
moment. Your boss hands you $1,000 at the end of the
year. You are delighted because you are expecting nothing. But suppose he had told you that he was going to give
you $10,000 and changed his mind? The same is true of
Youngman's wife — or anybody's spouse. Our standards
for other people are very different: actions that are attractive in others might be judged unattractive in a spouse.
Comparisons span everything from judgments of primitive sensations like heaviness and heat to judgments of
social status.

We even judge the contents of our mind by comparison.

4. *Get to the point!*

The mental system determines the meaning of any event,
its relevance to the person. In the process, it throws out
almost all the information that reaches us. Of the billions

of leaves you saw last summer, how many do you remember? A flash of red crossing your view may mean that your wife has driven home in her red car, but you hardly notice the visual stimulus, just its meaning. A siren is frightening because it *means* that the police want you to stop.

All these "policies" and procedures exist to simplify the amount of information current in the mind. "What have you done for me lately?" allows a focus on recent events. "Don't call me" allows many of the real changes in the world to go ignored.

I am leaving out number 3 — "Compared to what?" — here, because I want to treat the extraordinary range of comparative processes later in the book.

Number 4, "Get to the point!," allows us to operate on and to remember only the meaning of conversations, meetings, and different situations. "You mean you talked for three hours and you only decided to paint the house blue?"

This policy helps to simplify the load of the mind further: when something is meaningful it is organized; when it is organized, it is simplified in the mind.

If you look at a photograph, you will at first see many, many dots, and if you try to recall it, it will be difficult to keep the position of all the dots in mind. But when you organize it, it becomes simpler, and you can remember it later as "the grainy picture of the Dalmatian in the field." Studies of chess masters show the same thing: a position that to someone like me seems like a bunch of pieces strewn about the board to a master is instantly organized as Ruy Lopez 22. Once so organized, he knows where everything is. All these policies keep our minds relatively uncluttered.

Our own understanding of ourselves is also processed by the same routine, so we don't always know ourselves directly. We hold a well-organized and simplified version of our environment, of the nature of other people, and even of our own lives and our own beliefs in our minds.

This routine goes on "behind the scenes" of the mind. We are aware of the specific contents of the mind, but we are usually unaware of all the wheeling and dealing, the assembling and disassembling, of the MOS. Therefore we are often unaware of how we are making judgments and decisions, some of which are often inappropriate, misplaced, or just wrong.

We may not like our limited brain-mind system. Rather, one particular part of the person may not approve of another part. In fact, to the TWIT mentality, much of the rest of the human mind is quite unacceptable! Certainly many people, especially philosophers, educators, and scientists, would think that the entire mind is different — more rational, less messy, more coherent, and more appealing — than it is.

We are animals with a brain and mental system primarily organized around a few basic necessities: keeping warm and safe, minding the body and organizing our actions around the short-term contingencies of our environment. It is the system that "got us here."

And it is radically different from what we believe it to be.

PART II

MIND ON BRAIN

How Far You Have Come

Originally, you were clay. From being mineral, you became vegetable. From vegetable, you became animal, and from animal, man. During these periods man did not know where he was going, but he was being taken on a long journey nonetheless. And you have to go through a hundred different worlds yet.

— Jalaludin Rumi

CHAPTER FOUR

The Basic Miracles, the Magical Transformations, and the Modules of the Mind

WE DO NOT possess a thoroughly modern mind, although we do live in a modern world.

Our mental apparatus is an amalgam of different circuits, of different priorities, and even of the evolutionary developments of different eras. The human brain, whose structures underlie the functioning of the mind, was not constructed of new elements. It is a compendium of circuits piled atop one another, each developed to serve a short-term purpose in millennia past. Evolution does not, unfortunately, work for the long term, but rather for the immediate exigencies of survival for individual animals.

Knowing the general structure of the brain provides the basis for our understanding the mind's operations; current evidence in neuroscience must also be given great weight.

The brain developed over a period of more than 500 million years. It is composed of quite separate structures that seem to be laid on top of each other, like a house being remodeled. So we do not have one single brain but a multilevel brain, built in different eras for different priorities. Many of these separate brains have, loosely speaking, "minds of their own": minds for alertness, for emotions, for danger, for comparing sensory information, for avoiding scarcity.

The human brain is in part archaic: its design is based on the ground plan and the neural mechanisms of primates and, before that, other mammals and, even before that, vertebrates. For example, the structure of the codfish's brain, developed millennia ago and unchanged since, contains many of the basic elements of the human brain. The codfish even possesses a cerebral cortex (although it is small), a pituitary gland for controlling hormone production, and a cerebellum. In turn, vertebrates like codfish accepted many of their neural circuits and routines from much earlier and much simpler multicelled creatures.

Many of our commonplace preferences stem from the archaic nature of the nervous system. Our bodies try to return to the *milieu interieur* of those ancestors from the ocean, and we maintain concentrations of trace minerals in our internal fluids that would be appropriate in a fish living deep in the middle of the Mediterranean. We like weather that is approximately that of the East African plains, from which our first true ancestors came: between 60°F and 85°F, if possible.

We experience a work slump in the late afternoon because of the ancient body rhythms of our savanna-dwelling precursors. That was when they took their rest period; but in Norway in November, the same slump is there.

The cerebral hemispheres of the human brain control the opposite sides of the body because, hundreds of millions of years ago, simple creatures evolved specialized programs, stored in nerve nets, to move away from an attack. But if the attack and the means of movement had been on the same side, the creatures would have been unable to get away. So the nerves on the protected side of

the organism, opposite the attack, developed the ability to
sense information and to move the body away. Millions of
years later, this principle, with elaborate crossovers in the
nervous system, persists.

Our hackles get raised during a business meeting because our ancestors fluffed up their hairs in order to appear larger, more powerful, and more menacing to an
attacker. We raise gooseflesh to provide an insulating layer
of air in our fur—in fur that disappeared millions of years
ago. It is a response that would make us look larger to an
attacker if we were frightened.

The basic mechanisms of neural action and neurotransmission are identical in all mammals. We are so similar to
other animals that many different ones can serve as laboratory models for the human brain. The crawfish can be
used as a model of neurotransmission, the pig has a similar
capacity for learning, and even complex visual processes
can be studied using the cat or the rhesus monkey's occip-
ital cortex.

The same neural processes that were originally developed to judge brightness, taste, and weight now judge prices,
politics, and personalities.

In the very beginning of the machinery of the mind,
out there in the sensory system, the MOS policies are embodied in the design of the neural circuits: there is much,
much less transmitted to the brain than exists in the world
outside. The senses are the brain's outposts, and they receive signals from the external world to be transformed
into internal, psychological experience. They are not perfect windows on the outside, as is ordinarily assumed, but
almost the reverse. There is not much need for the sensory
systems to reflect all outside occurrences, but merely to
convey a few things that signify important information,
usually about changes in the state of an object or perhaps

an animal. These systems are a good example of the MOS policy of "Don't call me unless something new happens."

Sending only the limited amount of change information is the first and perhaps the most radical simplification of the mental system. The eye, the inroad to the most complex and rich dimension of our experience, transmits less than *one trillionth* of the information reaching its surface! We obviously cannot see what is really out there.

Due to the way the nervous system operates, most sensory experiences are not absolute but relative: their basic mode of action is to send information in comparison with previous experiences. If there is no change, comparatively, we don't see or hear anything. Constant noises disappear into the background, as do other constant sensations. Are you aware of your breathing now? Or the weight of your body against the chair? You are when I mention it, but since there is no "news," no sharp changes, it continues, and we don't need to be "called."

Our experiences of the world are composed of things brighter, darker, heavier, lighter, or sweeter than other things. The senses do not reflect the outside world completely; they discard most of the information. Equal changes in physical intensity do not produce equal changes in experience: the relationship between the internal and external worlds is not a simple one. A single candle flame emits a fixed amount of physical energy, but its experience depends on the surrounding circumstances. In a dark room, it allows us to see; in a bright room, it is hardly noticed.

When danger is approaching, the important thing to know is how fast it is approaching, not merely how much louder one threatening sound is than another. It is a simple and elegant solution to the problem of how we, or another animal, can keep track of all the things going on around us. The solution seems to be to select only things that change radically in comparison. It is a simple and brilliantly sensible beginning for the mental operating system, but it does give us trouble later on.

A system built to notice comparative differences provides flexibility and makes evolutionary sense. A sensory psychologist describes the use of the system thus: "Imagine yourself sitting in front of a fire surrounded by forests, without any effective weapons, listening to the growls of a large and hungry animal. The most important information would be the ratio between the loudness of two successive growls. If the present growl is twice as loud as the last one, you know that the animal has covered half the distance toward you in that time. So you know that it will be arriving in just about that much time!"

One of the most important limitations on our brain and mind comes from the constraints of physical space: there isn't room inside our heads for all the complex processing we would like or that we imagine we have.

Consider the basic process of interpreting colors. We can judge millions of different shades, hues, and brightnesses with a small set of circuits that needs to hold only comparative information. Otherwise, the color processing information of a human being might need a trailer full of brain cells carried behind! This economy of mind usually works well: with a very limited capacity we are able to see sunsets, fruit ripening on trees far away, the grays of the winter sky, and much more. And it takes psychological demonstrations to make us aware of how we respond differently to the same colors, depending upon the surroundings.

In this illustration, all the central squares are exactly the same gray, but the darker the surrounding figure, the brighter each square appears. An edge or corner or sharp change in color is a clear demarcation between two objects

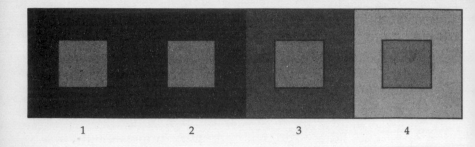

Simultaneous Brightness Contrast Fools Your Eye

or planes. The demarcation comes because it is at the point where a significant difference or contrast in brightness is noticed.

Things appear brighter at edges and corners than in the middle. The MOS works, not only to compare and enhance small changes, but also to select different kinds of information and then to enhance them for ease of action. Different organisms then would have different worlds as determined by the individual sensory-brain hardware, each one different in the service of the survival of the animal.

The great psychologist William James compared the selection processes of the mind to those of a sculptor carving a statue out of marble. This procedure involves many separate operations of whittling down the original huge object to a form that is individual.

We can see that the mind is at every stage a theatre of simultaneous possibilities. Consciousness consists in the comparison of these with each other, the selection of some, and the suppression of others, of the rest by the reinforcing and inhibiting agency of attention. The highest and most celebrated mental products are filtered from the data chosen by the faculty below that, which mass was in turn sifted from a still larger amount of simpler material, and so on. The mind, in short, works on his block of stone. In a sense, the statue stood there from eternity. But there were a thousand different ones beside it. The sculptor alone is to thank for having extracted this one from the rest. . . . Other minds, other worlds, from the same monotonous and inexpressive chaos! My world is but one in a million, alike embedded and alike real to those who may abstract them. How different must be the world in the *consciousness* of ants, cuttle fish, or crab!

Although I have quoted this passage often and admired as always James's eloquence, until something happened to me in an unexpected situation, I can't say that I genuinely felt the real differences in the different worlds of animals with which we live side by side. It seemed so obvious that there was one external reality out there! I was usually no better at breaking that illusion than those who concentrate solely on "fine thought" and argument.

But I was lucky to meet some squirrels under unusual circumstances.

I live in a house called pre-earthquake by real estate agents in California. This means (as far as I can manage a direct translation from real estate lingo) that the house is not only old but all wood. Most important for our story, it was for a long time plagued by squirrels. They liked to nest under the eaves of the roof and hold meetings in the recesses of the attic. They also liked to make fine meals of the sides of the house.

For at least ten years I harbored completely destructive

thoughts about them — torture, burnings, sending away for recipes for squirrel chili, and so on. Then I read an advertisement for a Rodent Eliminator, which quite gaily promised that it would "rid you once and for all of those pesty varmints and rodents." My order was in the afternoon mail.

I waited daily for the box to arrive.

It finally came. It was not, as I had imagined, a giant flame thrower or a miniature electric chair but a sealed small box with an on-off switch. The instructions advised to set the box near the rodents and "watch the rodents disappear forever." My hopes were high, and I followed the instructions somewhat nervously.

When I turned the machine on, nothing seemed to happen — nothing as far as I could see, anyway. Suddenly, however, there was a great, scurrying commotion. The squirrels were actually running over one another to get out. So many were trying to get out that they had to eat a new hole in the house to do so. Even so, I was delighted.

The Rodent Eliminator worked by generating a very high frequency wave in the air, one that is beyond the range of human sensitivity but within that of most rodents.

So, our worlds are different: I heard and felt nothing; the squirrels, in the words of the somewhat feverish manual, "will feel that a 747 jet has landed inside their heads." No 747 for me, and now no squirrels, either. I wished more than once that William James had had squirrels, too, and had lived long enough to use the eliminator.

The mental operating system creates and maintains our outside world, a world in which we can act and survive. *Our world appears to us the way it does because we are built the way we are.*

Consider yourself and a cat, both looking at a chocolate

cake. You see a brown cake and can taste its sweetness. The cat, however, does not see colors and cannot taste sweetness. A cat can, however, see things at night that you cannot because a reflective layer in its eye doubles the intensity of the light.

Other neural circuits in the sensory part of the MOS exaggerate changes in the world. This reduces our choice of actions to a tolerable level and registers priorities quickly. A loud noise gets us mobilized automatically; the sudden appearance of smoke does the same.

However, not every kind of information has the same kind of internal representation in us or in other animals. We ignore some things and respond quite strongly to others. Most of this is not deliberate but just the built-in characteristics of the primitive circuits of mind.

Look at these curves, which are technical graphs showing the internal transformations of three different kinds of information: distance, brightness, and pain. You will notice their different shapes. Let's look at distance. The plot shows that the external distance is mapped accurately inside, and as things get longer outside, there is an equal and corresponding increase in our internal experience of it. This is how we might imagine everything works inside our minds, but this is not so.

Look at the curve for brightness; as the brightness (actually the luminance) outside increases, there is not a consistent increase in the perceived brightness. The experience of brightness increases quickly at first, then slows as more luminance is added. As before, the candle added to a well-lit boardroom is all but invisible. Extremely bright things are muted in the mind.

Pain is represented in the opposite way from brightness: as pain stimuli increase, there are greater increases inside. The experience of pain is exaggerated: it has a physical

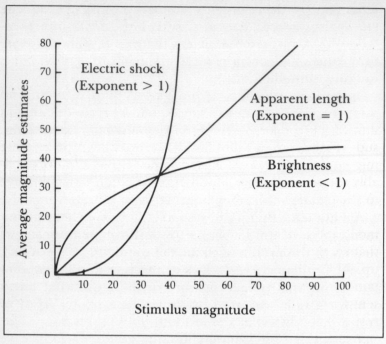

Power Curves for Different Stimuli

fast path into the brain, and it pre-empts other activities. In the words of Linus (of "Peanuts" renown): "Pain hurts!" So sudden pain will automatically and completely interrupt philosophical dialogue. A similar longing for food eventually breaks our concentration; disturbances — say, in the weather — that disrupt brain functions can also disrupt thought. Our biology gives our mental processes priorities, some of which are strong and obvious such as this one, some of which are more subtle and pervasive, which we will encounter later.

The contents of the mind are a mixture of thoughts, ideas, sensations, and fantasies. Images appear and go;

ideas emerge fleetingly only to disappear again; an ache or a pain surfaces, then a desire. This mental representation is successful to the extent that we survive. But as we now know, it is not a complete version of reality, but a radically simplified one.

The MOS serves to govern the safety of the person. And safety requires constant monitoring of local conditions and immediate concerns — danger approaching, scarce food, sudden shifts in the weather. So our mind produces what might be called the small, short view. Otherwise, we probably would not know what to do in a crisis. We would have to sift through too many alternatives.

All human beings are similarly evolved to select common aspects of the physical surroundings: we possess eyes that receive radiant electromagnetic energy, ears that pick up the mechanical vibrations of the air, a nose that contains receptors for gaseous molecules, specialized touch sensors, and a complex of cells on the tongue shaped to respond to the molecules in food.

We "touch" only what we need to get by, just as a cat's whiskers touch only those spaces which are too small to enter. It's the "What have you done for me lately" and "Don't call unless something new happens" policies, already wired up in the sensory systems.

The senses begin the first great transformation of outside information into the small world of the mind. There are such a great number of routine miracles in this system that are dazzling to contemplate from "the outside": a selection of a very few of the very short waves in the air becomes a painting in the mind; longer ones become music. It is all done within ourselves, and done at every moment of every day.

Miracle-shmiracle, it still does not get us anywhere in the world. Pressure waves in the air are converted to volleys of neural firing, minuscule waves are converted to color, but how can we tell whether someone is speaking or if it is just noise, how can we tell if the color is from an object that we know or is just a streak on the horizon, needing no action?

This next level of analysis is the data-processing part of the mind. This kind of analysis occurs, of course, after the data selection of the senses and operates on the transformed sensory information. It all happens in the cortex of the brain.

It is thought that here exist specific modules of connected neurons in the brain which analyze the raw incoming sensory information. A volley of neural firing stemming from the ear is analyzed into a set of words and an identification of the speaker; a transmission of firing from the visual system is further transformed into a cup being rotated; pressure information is translated into the movement of a cat on our arm.

These modules are thought to be relatively innate and to serve only the information in one sensory system: language probably has a different kind of analysis routing from form; smell probably has its own module, which is different from pressure. These systems probably evolved at different eras for different purposes.

The cortex is built in a quite interesting manner, with specialized cells arranged in columns that seem to have specific functions, such as the detection of corners or edges in the visual system. These standard ("hard-wired," to the trade) data-processing centers in the cortex and below serve as modules for the basic interpretation of information.

These modules do the basic analytical work of the mind: translating a pattern of sounds into language; determining from millions of bits of visual information whether this is the same train; decoding a set of squiggles to give us the important and abstract mathematical symbols like 1, 89, and >; keeping track of the position of the limbs in order to avoid a dog; and much more. There are probably modules for specific reactions and patterns of activity, too.

Important components of the mind, probably existing in the same kind of modular structure, are prepared associations, connections between items in the world. To the empiricists since Locke, the viewpoint has been that any learning is due to experience, and anything can just as easily be learnt as anything else.

However, there are obviously some things that are easy to learn and hard to forget. The strong experience of pain is quite difficult to dissociate from where the pain occurred. Have you ever, for instance, been driving and had an accident? It is certainly much harder to go right back to the wheel than usual. Strong fears can shade into phobias (the Greek word for "fears") and prevent you from rejoining life. But if you analyze most phobias, you find that they often concern items that are a real threat to safety. While a Freudian can make much of fear of snakes, for instance, snakes have been a danger for most of human history. And what of spiders, or vermin? Why do many people fear them? Obviously, many of our reactions are built in to the brain in a modular fashion, and they can impede cognition as well.

So it is important to note that we seem to have evolved a set of special analyzing mechanisms for the different problems our ancestors encountered. Early in evolution, when sophisticated movement control was needed, the cerebellum was stuck aside the brainstem. In the next chapter we will see that when we needed to live on land, an area of the brain developed to handle the necessary contingencies. And language, too, evolved in a specific part of the brain.

Further, there seem to be specific kinds of modular action programs, probably specific to each species, that handle special situations. We mobilize in response to scarce resources and in times of emergency. We react strongly to any kind of food upset and remember to avoid it.

This is how we, and all animals, get the information we need to survive. These processes exist within in the initial circuits of the eyes, ears, and nose, and they extend all the way up to the data-processing modules in the brain.

Our primary analysis system is enormously sophisticated. It produces a representation of the complex world we experience with a few general procedures: a radical and limited selection of information related to survival; the further simplification by the transmission of only a comparison of that information; and it feeds information into the next level of the mind, the decision and thought centers of the brain.

These same policies of the senses are still in operation millions of years later!

CHAPTER FIVE

Piece of Mind 1:
On the Patchwork Quilt
of Talents in the Brain

I INTRODUCED this book by saying that there is a common progression in discovery. First impressions of an unknown entity are usually oversimplified; with later investigation, our impressions become more detailed and complex. This has happened in understanding the nature of the mind: early single-minded views have been superseded by more complex views; and it has also occurred in our understanding of the structure and functioning of the human brain. It is only in the past four decades that the study of the brain has progressed beyond inspired guesswork and wishful thinking.

This chapter is the first of three scattered through the book that describe the different pieces of the mind that have been identified. Here we consider the concentration in the brain of centers of talents. These talents are one of the primary biological components of the "small minds" that are active at any one time. In the next chapter I will try to review the story so far.

The brain is the most difficult "object" to study. The brain case itself seems, to the researcher, designed to shield the brain, not only from injuries to the person, but from the prying eyes of neuroscientists. And when you finally try to "enter" the brain, its structure, almost invisible at the best of times, seems to have little to do with its operations. There are obvious relationships between biological structure and function. The heart looks like a pump and acts like one. The brain doesn't look like anything else and doesn't act like anything else.

Nevertheless, the revolutions in neurochemistry, the study of brain evolution, and neuroscience have all combined to give a new and radically different picture of the brain and the specialized centers within it.

The first and oldest two layers are concerned mainly with more and more complex processes of keeping alive; the third and newer part of the brain seems most specialized for creating anew — not only adapting to the world as it is found, but changing the world to adapt to the organism. A few hundred million years of this history in a few brief paragraphs now follow.

The oldest part of the brain is similar to the entire brain of many reptiles and looks like the brain of the crocodile. Called the brainstem, it evolved to its present state about 500 million years ago. It accounts largely for our general alertness and the basic mechanisms of life support. It lies below much of the later developments of evolution, and although basic life support is of some importance to us, it is not the locus of much of the activities we consider "mind."

On top of the brainstem is the limbic system, which presided over the transition from sea-dwelling to land animals and reached its current state of development about 200 million years ago. It is different in appearance, different in structure, and different in the kinds of neural activity it contains. In order to exist on land, a new kind of brain

had to evolve, body temperature and thirst had to be placed
under precise regulation, and reactions to danger had to
be programmed, as these needs are more of a problem on
land than in the sea.

Along with this quite precise and new kind of brain also
came food and weight regulation, the great expansion of
emotional reactions, the responses to emergencies, and
many of the complex actions that ensure survival in the
much more diverse and challenging circumstances encountered by land mammals. Many of the developments
of the limbic system are still with us today, as we have
pretty much the same basic emotional apparatus as our
remote ancestors had.

The cortex was the last part of the brain to evolve. In
the cortex decisions are made, schemes are hatched, language is heard, music is written, mathematics is created.
The cortex is like a quilt that covers the rest of the brain;
it is folded so that it can fit within the small human head.
Our head must be small so that it can move through the
narrow birth canal of the mother. For this reason, the
head, its brain, and the rest of us must "escape" early
during gestation, and we are born with a relatively unfin-
ished brain. (It is only 25 percent of its adult weight.) The
human brain does most of its growing after birth, unlike
the brain of any other animal.

Certain normal experiences cause the innate abilities of
the cortex to develop, but the exact development depends
on the particular world of the child. Every normal human
being, for instance, learns to speak, but the particular language and the rules it learns depend on its culture. And
we lose certain abilities as we develop; the Japanese seem
to be unable to pronounce the English *R* if they are brought
up in Japan, but if brought up in America they can speak
well enough to become network newscasters.

In a sense, the discovery here has been easy, at least in terms of the straightforward interpretation of increasingly intricate experimental methods. And although there are the usual academic ragings about the interpretation of specific evidence, by normal standards the work has been straightforward.

The relationship of thought and other higher-level mental processes to the structure of the cortex has been more of a problem. Here much depends upon the interests and interpretations of the investigator, so this has been an area of much more controversy, which I have felt personally.

The first neurophysiologists (in the late nineteenth and early twentieth centuries) analyzed the brain as a single mass. To some of these early workers, even the most celebrated, the discovery of the single neuron was heretical, for the brain was thought to be a homogeneous, single unit. Nevertheless, with modern techniques it was determined that the brain had a complicated structure made up of billions of cells.

Yet even after the discovery of the neuron, the brain was still thought to act as a single system. Some of the first influential experiments on brain function and learning were done in the laboratory of Karl Lashley, a great physiologist. He proceeded to remove pieces of cortex and chart the effects on learning of simple associations. His work showed that the more cortex that was removed from an animal (in this case, a dog), the greater the impairment of the learning process.

So the earliest understanding of the brain was the simplest. First-generation neurophysiologists believed the brain, especially the cells of the cortex, to be "equipotential." Any part of the brain was thought to have an equal role in any action.

The early and influential learning theorists like B. F.

Skinner found this simplified understanding of the brain quite congenial. The contemporary doctrine of learning (following Locke) held that anything could be conditioned as easily as anything else. The brain could be considered a single system and everything in the mind was equal. The behaviorists, may they rest in peace, would have hated that term, but such was their approach.

The primitive and simplified physiology arising from these investigations was well in accord with contemporary social movements and political theorizing, especially among the academically respectable in America. This view of learning and of the brain was eagerly promoted to accord with the generally optimistic approach in American education. While the social aims of equality of opportunity are quite laudable, the idea of equality of ability was mistaken.

The viewpoint of, to be only a little silly, "a single and equal brain for all" was an important idea politically. The excitement of the idea that anyone could learn anything did enhance the quality of the work that went into education. It provided an acceptable physiological rejoinder to the much more idiotic and brutal genetic determinism rationale that was coming from the physicians and theorists of Nazi Germany. Even today, in the United States, mentioning the influence of the inheritance of specific abilities can call up immediate cries of fascism in those who have better intentions than education.

But we are not equal in capacity, it is obvious to anyone that people differ in many respects: their preference for visual or auditory information, their ability to read, to skate, to reason, to place the right color in a picture, to drive, to add, and much more. So, and sadly for my generation of psychologists and educators, we have finally recognized that we are never dealing with a standard individual with a standard mind. Even now there is a kind of embargo on such discussions because of the association of genetic differences with the disgraceful use of genetics by the Nazis and the later antiblack propaganda, and there is the additional association of free society with a simple-minded view of the mind and brain.

I entered the study of mind and brain in the 1970s. I was exposed to some of the exciting developments in neuroscience in the 1960s, from the new work in EEG technology, work on dividing the brain (from the future Nobel laureate Roger Sperry's lab) to countless studies of the circuitry of the brain by many physiologists.

New methods, such as the use of microelectrodes and the beginnings of neurochemistry, opened a new era in the understanding of the brain. It was well known at that time that by "splitting the brain"—that is, by dividing it surgically (for the treatment of severe epilepsy) at the great cerebral commissure (a kind of monumental connecting cable between the two cerebral hemispheres)—you could produce a person with two separated spheres (well, hemispheres) of mind.

But is this the case with normal brains? Did much of the evidence, adduced for almost a century on the basis of brain damage, really represent average people? Were the split-brain phenomena themselves a product of the surgery or a product of the damaged brains of the severely impaired epileptics who were in desperation given experimental surgery?

We needed a method whereby thousands of people could be studied, people who were not clinical cases. I began to develop an EEG procedure so that the exciting studies based on a few surgical cases could be generalized to ordinary people. By recording the tiny electrical potentials on the scalp, my colleagues and I could show that most people activated and suppressed their hemispheres, one at a time, when they were reading or drawing, thinking critically or creatively, reading technical material or stories.

I characterized these two minds as rational and intuitive, the rational faculties depending predominantly upon left-hemisphere processes, the intuitive (immediate knowing of the environment) on the right. I think this view is still sometimes useful, but the scientific understanding of the brain has become more detailed and specific. The brain's complexity is much greater than just its major divisions. We have gone, now, far beyond the two-mind view to a many, or multimind view.

There are certainly more independent and smaller units of ability residing in the cortex, more segmented and specialized centers than we knew about in the late 1960s and early 1970s. While it still may be useful to categorize someone as using one or the other hemispheres predominantly (the potter who is interested in body movement and the lawyer who loves debating as a recreation come to mind), certainly we have gone further into the analysis of this problem using the vast evidence available to us over the past two decades.

Let us return to the separate centers of talents, stuck inside the cortex like patches in a folded quilt. While the evidence is hardly all in, I think we can begin to sketch the different "talent patches" in the brain. "Talent" is not the usual name, but I think its difference from ordinary neurological terminology will be helpful. I call certain well-defined anatomical centers talents because they are to some degree inherited (in the ordinary sense of God-given talents), because some people probably have more of one than another, and because these abilities — like the ability to move gracefully or to speak fluently — seem to form coherent mental and behavioral units as well as existing

as specific anatomical units. These talents are the next
level of neural organization beyond the modules. They
are, in the main, the recipients of the modules' data
analysis.

If you look at the brain this way, you will see it divided
into different and well-defined areas, each of which possesses a rich concentration of certain abilities. If marked,
they would look just like a set of patches on our folded
quilt.

The talents range from quite basic mental abilities, like
the memory for smells, to those considered high-level
functions, like determining the meaning of a poem. You
will not be surprised to find that the most basic talents
concern short-term survival; the more elaborate, abilities
like sports and movement; and the most complex, the sense
of self and thinking abilities.

The talents divide into different functions of the mind.
Here's a first list of those for which there are either reasonably well identified areas of the brain which are predominantly involved in specific activities or talents that are
clearly overall functions of the brain. I am under no illusion that these will prove to be the only talents we have or
that there could be no argument about these specific eleven
ones, but this list, wheeled in with the policies and the
modules, will do for a first try.

activating
informing
smelling
feeling
healing (probably a talent with less association to a partic-
    ular area than others)
moving
locating and identifying
calculating

talking
knowing
governing

First, and perhaps the most biologically similar among different people, are the activating talents: specific and identifiable centers of the brain regulate hunger and thirst and various kinds of appetites, from food to sex. Some people, however, are much more "driven" by factors outside their conscious control than others: to succeed at any cost, to get rich, to drink and eat often or well, to have sex. Many of these factors may well have strong representation in the limbic system as well as control from the cortex.

Clearly, too, these talents — although some may feel I am stretching it right at the beginning — are independent of one another in most people; appetites for food, water, or sex may be quite different within an individual and vary among people, although an appetite for one can often be satisfied by another.

Residing within this talent area of the brain are the forces that determine our weight, which seems to be regulated around a set point by the brain, so that it is quite difficult to gain or lose weight beyond the set point.

Also rather basic to the organism are the informing talents. To survive in the world, we must know what is happening inside and outside ourselves: noises must be monitored, movements of others seen and their future position calculated; our own limbs must be continuously monitored, as well as the state of the musculature and the presence or absence of pain. Pain is so important that there are two separate sensory networks of neurons that transmit pain information to the brain. One is a fast system, which sends information about sudden pains, like placing a hand on a hot plate. The other is a slow system, which conveys the constant aches and pains like that of the lower back.

All this information must be assembled and action taken. This is why informing is a talent closely based on the transformations and modules described in the previous chapter. We need to know what to do with the sensory information. Clearly, people differ in knowing what is going on inside and outside themselves: one woman was recently rushed to the hospital in spasms of stomach pain to discover that she was about to give birth. She didn't even know she was pregnant. For others, internal pains and upsets have strong access to consciousness and cannot be ignored. Sharpshooters often have extraordinary sensory acuity. Some people can discriminate between two tones, each of which may be inaudible to a person of average hearing.

Closely associated with informing but most likely the product of separate development is smelling. The physiology of the smell system is certainly anatomically separate from the others, as noted earlier. The nerves from the nose are unique in that they surge to the brain without any intermediate synapses. Smelling gives us our most direct experience of the world.

The memories for smell probably make up a separate mental system from those of other sensory and perceptual experiences. In both laboratory experiments and in life it is quite difficult to forget a smell once it is experienced. Even years later, say, in returning to a city, a memory seems to arise directly even though the smell seemed to be forgotten. I returned to Thailand recently after an absence of more than twenty years. Its particular sweet tropical smell — of the meat, of the lack of hygiene, of the fecund growth — made me feel as if I had never left, so dominating at that moment was this particular component of mind.

There are certainly virtuosos of smell: people who make their living judging perfumes, scents, and the "nose" of wines. Smells affect us strongly; they determine to a great extent what we eat and to some extent our attraction to other people. The smell of different people, some biologists believe, may be related to their tissue group, a complex determinant of the rejection of implants. It may be that a reproductive match is "read out" in smell somehow (but don't quote me on it). The attraction of others by their smell is, however, quite clear and provides yet another reason for thinking that smelling is a quite separate sensation.

There is at least one center of the talents of feeling which comprises basic and universal emotions like anger, fear, and sadness. It might be possible that the control of positive emotions like joy are separated in another center, but this is unknown at present. Some evidence divides generally positive and negative emotions into the left and right hemispheres respectively, suggesting that they may be under different control.

People clearly differ in the strength of their feelings, at least on how much and how often they may become emotional. They clearly also differ on the kind of emotion they may usually express, although I am inclined to regard the expression of the emotions as something more complicated than the basic experience of them. This expression is quite malleable: some people have no difficulty crying on cue in a play every night, whereas others find it very difficult to call up their feelings even in a poignant or joyous situation, let alone at will.

For some, the feeling dimension is the very basis of their lives; for others, it is something to be ignored. Those who ignore it are probably just fooling themselves, since our feelings toward most situations are what often determine our opinions, whether we admit it or not.

When Jimmy Carter debated Ronald Reagan for the presidency in 1980, most people felt that Reagan had won after seeing the debate, while most who read the transcripts felt Carter had won. Reagan became president because he projected more positive feelings, which is what the voting public wanted. The same is true about television comedy shows in general. When the canned laughter is removed, we laugh less and like the show less, even though we believe we don't like the canned laughter.

The basic job of the brain is healing. It is, as a whole, a health machine. It monitors the heart, lungs, and the actions of all the glands and organs. It governs digestion, elimination, secretion, and immunity to diseases (the brain is intimately connected to the immune system). Most of the other activities of the brain—the sensing of internal and external worlds, our feelings, our abilities to move—all serve the purpose of providing nourishment, incorporating it, eliminating toxic substances, and avoiding injury or illness. This is why I do not feel the need to identify healing with only one specific area of the cortex.

It is most tragic to see this talent of the brain degenerate, for the rest goes with it, and equally tragic are those rare people born without the basic mechanisms of healing, like the guidance of the immune system. There are social and mental factors in healing as well: those who have many friends have less illness. That the brain is a health system and that healing is a real talent are just being understood as the understanding of the physiology of the brain progresses and the psychological factors of illness and disease are discovered. Sadness affects immunity; loneliness can cause a broken heart; self-centeredness, in the ordinary sense of the word, can contribute to heart disease.

The immense job of moving first involves the coordination of the many sights, sounds, colors, tastes, internal sensations, and our own movements. This ability resides more clearly and completely in the cortex than do the emotional talents. It consists of a narrow band of specialized neurons in the central cortex which receive the information from the senses and transform it into movements — a sensory-motor strip, as it is often termed. For instance, look at a baby trying to walk and try to remember the difficulty of moving an arm, a leg, another one, looking in the distance and at your feet. Some people seem to lack a sense of body position and coordination forever. (Sometimes, although rarely, this problem can be pathological.) They can't even locate their own body and may find it difficult to dress after some forms of brain injury to these areas.

And there can be little argument about the word "talent" for this one! I can refer you to the public works of a certain Dr. Julius Erving of Philadelphia or of Mikhail Baryshnikov of Washington for a demonstration of these abilities. Sportscasters and writers are closer to the truth than the TWITs when they call a move in a game brilliant. It is a separate ability to be able to move with grace and to anticipate, in sports and in perhaps hunting, the moves of others. It does not reduce to words, to sounds, or to smells. It has nothing to do with appetite or the ability to read. It is just a move mind, there on its own.

While this has been the subject of endless challenges and debate among many in brain science, it is clear that there are important divisions in the brain. Both hemispheres of

the cerebral cortex seem to have a special concentration
of talents, at least in most people.

Several of the right-hemisphere talents include those of
locating and identifying functions that involve space, place,
and face.

Space is quite important to us. It is as simple, too, as the
ability to move a large sofa around a corner into a small
room. Doing this can be a vexing problem for some people, while for others it requires no effort at all. A sym-
phony conductor may be brilliant in concert but may well
be stymied at the problem of the sofa. It is easy for some
people to appreciate, respond to, or even produce sculpture, while its meaning and even its language are incom-
prehensible to others. To do sculpture or to appreciate
the forms created and to be able to work at carpentry and
architecture also require spatial abilities.

Closely allied but probably independent is the ability of
place. The need to know where one is is quite basic—how
to retrace the route along which one has moved, how to
return home. Put some of those with place talents in a new
city and they immediately know how to get to the mu-
seums or to the best restaurants (depending, of course, on
the strength of their activating preferences!).

Those so gifted need little instruction in telling their left
from their right, where north and west are, while for others
it is embarrassing: they cannot find the fish store they have
been to seventy times. A distinguished professor of my
acquaintance cannot bring himself to ask for proper di-
rections because he cannot read maps. Left-handed people and their relatives seem to have more of a disturbance
in this ability than others.

To recognize people by their faces is an important and
immediate ability, which most of us have. We seem to be
able to remember a face but not necessarily a name, as the

cliché has it, because these are different abilities, lodged differently. It is important to know whether we have seen someone before—it was probably more important in primitive societies than now—and it is clearly important to be able to recognize the language of the face, the emotions that are expressed primarily by the facial musculature.

This ability is clearly innate; it appears quite early if not immediately in development with almost no prodding. It evidently depends on some extremely complex circuitry in the parietal lobes. Think, for instance, of the enormous number of people you see in the street and the ease with which you recognize someone whom you were not expecting to see, perhaps whom you have not seen in several years. However, brain damage, especially in the parietal lobes, can yield the condition of *prosopagnosia*, the inability to recognize faces.

A quite striking talent is that of calculating. We calculate constantly: on the rate of movement of objects around us, on our own movements, on quantities of weight and brightness we experience. Our actions are constantly based on our calculation of the effort expended and the gains obtained. We take short cuts to save time, we spend less when we can, we rearrange our heavy work so as to expend less effort.

A much higher and much later development of calculation is in formal mathematics. This talent is, I believe, independent of others that might seem intellectual, such as verbal fluency or even logic. Instead, great leaps in mathematics are often made by people who do not do well in other areas but seem to spring on the scene, almost untutored, at a very young age. One survey of mathematical genius showed that most mathematicians made their great contributions by their mid-twenties. Mathematics seems to have a stronger spatial component, and less of a verbal one, than most people think.

While the undoubted talent of talking seems to be the closest to the single-minded idea of intelligence, it is clear that there are at least two separate areas of the left hemisphere that control our understanding of words and their production.

Damage to each of the areas also produces quite different kinds of aphasia, the loss of language. The first specific area of the brain to be identified with a specific talent was Broca's area in the left hemisphere. Damage here seems to destroy the fluency of speech but not the ability to convey meaning. The person simply no longer has the ability to select the words to express his thought.

In his classic study of the effects of brain damage on the mind, *The Shattered Mind,* the psychologist Howard Gardner describes an interview with a coast guard operator.

"Were you in the Coast Guard?"
"No, er, yes,
yes . . . ship . . . Massachu . . . chusetts
Coastguard . . . years."
He raised his hands twice, indicating the number nineteen.
"Oh, you were in the Coast Guard for nineteen years."
"Oh . . . boy . . . right . . . right."

This was the speech of a man who had normal speech before his left-hemisphere injury. He clearly wanted to communicate but could not do it.

That there are clearly separated verbal abilities is shown by another sort of brain injury to a different portion of the left hemisphere. The tragic result is called Wernicke's aphasia. Again Gardner comments:

"What brings you to the hospital?" I asked the 72-year-old

retired butcher four weeks after his admission to the hospital.

"Boy, I'm sweating, I'm awful nervous, you know, once in a while I get caught up, I can't mention the tarripoi, a month ago, quite a while. I've done a lot well, I impose a lot, while, on the other hand, you know what I mean, I have to run around, look it over, trebbin and all that sort of stuff."

I attempted several times to break in, but was unable to do so against this relentlessly steady and rapid outflow . . .

"Thank you, Mr. Gorgan, I want to ask you a few —

"Oh sure, go ahead, any old think you want. If I could I would. Oh, I'm taking the word the wrong way to say, all of the barbers here whenever they stop you it's going around and around, if you know what I mean, that is tying and tying for repucer, repuceration, well, we were trying the best that we could while another time it was with the beds over there the same thing."

In one case, the words cannot carry the meaning; in another, the words carry no meaning but sound coherent, although unbridled by any direction. These are probably two separate verbal talents: producing the words and producing the meaning.

Decoding the meaning of spoken words is a separate ability. By decoding I do not mean the lower-level module of analyzing the sounds in order to make them speech, but knowing what the speaker's words mean.

For instance, the sentence "He spread the warm bread with jam" occasions little reaction. It is automatically analyzed and registered. However, consider listening to this sentence: "He spread the warm bread with socks." This one causes a gigantic leap in the activity of the brain just after the sentence is completed.

Obviously we know that *socks* does not fit the normal expectations of the sentence, although it is not a surprising word to find. While the decoding module is adequate to produce a basic understanding of the words from the transformed sensory input, real talent is required to know what they mean. In a more ordinary example, "It's hot in here" can mean one thing if it is an object of desire who says it or another if your boss is commenting on your responsibilities as building supervisor.

So, associated with the talent of talking is listening and understanding speech. The ability to interpret speech depends first on the lower-level modular analyses but also on the interpretations and inferences of the more flexible knowledge centers higher up in the brain.

Reading and writing are probably not talents in the sense of this chapter. Every human being without significant brain damage or devastating experiences (like being raised by wolves) can talk and understand speech. But not everyone is literate. Writing and reading must be taught through a specific program of instruction and are certainly secondary abilities.

There seem, too, to be specific centers of knowing in the brain. There are at least two separate talents here, and most likely there are more. One, concerned with fine detail, is in the left hemisphere; another, which connects observations into a whole, is in the right.

The detailed processing of logical analysis seems to be separate from the talent of talking and separate, too, from mathematics. The ability to reason, to make critical inferences, can be destroyed by brain damage or stroke, although it is clearly not as organized an area as is the ability to string words together.

In addition to logical analysis, there seems to be the intuitive or overall form center. This consists of the ability to determine where the disconnected pieces of a puzzle (be they literal or metaphorical) fit together and how elements such as unconnected line lengths come together to make a square. Many people seem to know, without regard to inferences, how to pick the right stock, how to buy the right house at the right time. It is not currently academically popular to posit this as an ability, but this particular talent is not one that is strongly represented in most of the academic world; it is the talent of the artist and the money manager, not the art dealer and the accountant.

Somewhere in the brain, these pieces get assembled by a uniquely human talent, the governing talent of the self, a talent that takes precedence over the others. I think it comes above the others because its job is organizing the information that is produced by the other talents and by the modules. The functions of this talent are organization, inference, and interpretation and control.

Some functions of the self depend chiefly on the functions of the frontal lobes. These lobes lie at the intersection of the neural pathways that convey information from the rear portions of the brain, about other people, and information from the limbic system, about one's own state.

Here, probably, we assemble many of the inferences and the calculations we have about ourselves and our own representation of ourselves. Damage to certain parts of the frontal areas results in the inability to carry out our plans and the normal routines of daily life. In some cases, damage to this area even interferes with our ability to know on a long-term basis who we are. We may well be able to carry out complex activities almost as normal, but not know why we are doing them — why we are paying bills, why a group of people are gathered together for a birthday party, and the like.

Some of the functional abilities of this governing self talent are: observing the actions of the person; inferring about the nature of the outside world and the person himself; planning courses of actions. And perhaps the most complex functions are the governing acts: commanding the different components of mind.

The human self is different from that of other animals; many philosophers write that other animals don't have a self. I can't answer that, but I know there is a point in development when a young child can recognize itself. This has been demonstrated by a clever experiment. If you put a clownlike red dot on the forehead of a baby and place him before a mirror, he does not treat the image with a dot any differently from any other image in the mirror. When the child is a little older, he begins to notice that it is he with the dot, and he begins to touch it and to look at himself differently. At the same time, the child shows a concern with how he appears and what he does, and whether he makes a mistake. He has some self-awareness.

We also have what psychologists are unfortunately calling metacognition, our knowledge of what is in our mind. It is important for us to know what we know. What was Aristotle's profession? What was his major work? In what country did he live? What was his address? What was his telephone number? You know immediately that the answer to the last question is not in your mind.

This faculty probably appeared with the emergence of the ability to plan, to infer, and to abstract information. It became elaborated late in evolution, probably during the emergence of modern man, the period of the rapid cortical growth of the past 4 million years.

This separate part of the brain integrates information about the qualities of the person it resides in. This is, admittedly, a very different view: in this new understanding of the brain, the self is one of many components of the mind, independent of the rest of the mind, and must calculate its own conclusions, rightly or wrongly, about its person. I am using this weird terminology because there is a quite radical and quite counter-intuitive position about the multimind here. We do not have special or direct access to what is going on inside ourselves: often we guess, infer, or calculate it.

We do not have the same information about others that we do about ourselves. We have both special and limited access to ourselves. On the one hand, we have great and extensive experience of us. This governing center is always around as we think, sleep, and act well and badly. The self has access to difficulties and extenuating circumstances that it does not have about others.

Because of this our judgments are automatically biased; we tend to attribute the actions of others to their general characteristics and our own actions to the particular situation. When someone cuts in front of you in line for the cinema, he is automatically considered rude. When you do it, it is because you are rushing to get the seat for your child, who may be very hurt and disappointed if he does not get to see the show.

In other ways, too, we do not hear or observe ourselves the way we experience others. Have you ever listened to your own voice on tape? Chances are that it seemed too squeaky and high-pitched. But you are wrong. You just don't usually hear it.

So we don't "know thyself" in the normal way in which the brain is built. In fact, we have built-in illusions, from our voices to our easy explanation of our behavior. Thus questions such as "Do we know directly what we feel?" are not answered by a simple yes or no. The answer may depend on the understanding of the "we" in the question.

The emotional part of the brain may well know what it feels, but the rest of the mind usually must make separate inferences about it. The inferences may be simple misunderstandings, such as any two people might have in their interpretations of events, or they may well be deliberate distortions and screening of information. A feeling of strong attraction to someone forbidden may be interpreted as strong dislike in order to forestall the attraction. Certainly, information can be in one or another part of the mind and may well be shunted from one to another.

"I know my own mind" is an idea we often have. Or we may say, "My mind's made up about this." It seems reasonable that we should know our own mind, and we do, certainly better than others. But we don't know it directly or very well, with any more ease or precision than we know how our pancreas is functioning. "Know thyself" is probably more difficult than we had imagined, Plato excepted.

But the self does have a special place. It contributes most to the top level of the mind, the controlling functions of consciousness. Our ordinary speech is close to an accurate description here, as we speak of self-consciousness, self-understanding, and self-observation as important talents and disabling factors in a person's makeup.

But the self, although possessing a privileged place in the mind, is more isolated than we would have ordinarily imagined. It is just another independent talent of the mind, located in a specific portion of the brain. It has less special access to other equally important parts of the brain than we think. It is just doing its own job.

These talents and abilities of the mind, then, can operate independently and be combined into larger units, as members of a team may get called onto the field. The abilities of space and logic are needed to run an architectural business. The emotional and the movement talents may combine in expressive dance. The protective aspects of the emotions and logic may join to form paranoia. We can think of hundreds of likely combinations.

The lack of a talent may be crucial. The underdevelopment of certain kinds of emotional reactions may contribute to antisocial behavior, even criminality. Talents are one of the important basic units of the mind's operations, I believe.

CHAPTER SIX

Multimind Described

WE ARE MUCH more complex and much more intricate than we imagine. There is a different structure to the mind than we think, and there are many different levels of operation of the mind. Some are quite fixed and rigid, some flexible, some innate, some learned. Some have direct access to consciousness, some do not. No wonder we have been so confused and have asked questions about the mind that pertain to different levels. The multimind view is a multilevel or hierarchical view of the mind.

At the most elementary level, the one most similar in almost all animals, there are basic neural processes that transform incoming information from its raw form to a form manageable by the brain. We don't *see* anything directly. Here's what must happen: information, say, in the form of electromagnetic radiation in the "light" band, must first be transduced into the language of the brain, neural firing, by the retina and the visual system. While this process in all sensory systems is basic and relatively hard-wired, we still consider it a miracle, one that goes on each moment of our life.

After the miracles, the transformed information still must

be converted further into something sensible. The various pressure waves in the air may be converted into the neural language of sound, but what is being said, or is anything being said? Is an utterance in the language of the speaker; is it Polish or Japanese? This occurs in each system by separate data-processing modules that are probably specific to each sense: hearing sounds and hearing speech; vision; smell; touch; taste.

In these modules, extraction of meaning from converted sounds takes place: the consistent perception of red under bright sunlight and dusk; the realization that a building that now is blocking our view is the same building as one that appears as a speck three miles away. These and more probably have their own private special computational modules designed to extract information. These are the quick and stupid analytical systems of the mind. In my view they are not flexible but do a lot of automatic dirty work for us.

These modules provide the basic information for the talents of the mind just described, all of which ordinarily operate under the general policies briefly described in Chapter 3. The talents and the lesser abilities are slower and brighter than the modules. They are much more general, more flexible, and have much more capacity for change than do the modules. If you think about it, it is a good system; we can automatically respond to much of what goes on in the world and also have several higher-level capacities to evaluate and act on that kind of response and, when necessary, to override the automatic analysis.

But—and here is where the modern understanding of the brain and consciousness come in—*we do not have access to all of our talents at once*. Our consciousness is clearly limited to only a few items at a time. This is why the system comprises an uncountable number of small minds. These are the talents, parts of the talents, the modules, and the policies.

We wheel in and out of consciousness a certain number of these small minds to handle different situations in our lives. The particular combination of them that we possess and employ is probably what other people mean by personality.

However, we can never operate with a "full deck" but with only a small selection of the total mental apparatus at any one time. This means that all our faculties of mind are never available at once. So, at any one time we are much more limited, much more changeable, than we might otherwise believe of ourselves.

The levels of multimind, then, are, from the top down:

---

consciousness

"small minds"

the talents as described and smaller single abilities

the domain-specific data-processing modules

reflexes, set reactions
the basic neural transformations

The Policies: sensitivity to recent information; emphasis on vivid information; simplifying by comparison; focus on meaning—all influence activities at all levels.

The small minds that become active are thus specific to different situations and are quickly changed. One moment your mind might comprise a set reaction like the food avoidance program, and you find yourself not wanting to eat in a restaurant in which you were once poisoned. Or a general policy might swing in: you become extra careful about the chemical plant in your area after reading about the disaster in Bhopal, India. At one moment one talent like talking may fill the small mind, or the current small mind might join different talents or may involve a piece of each talent. It is not a consistent system.

Some small minds are more encompassing than others; they may well control many smaller small minds. The large biological units, like the limbic system and each hemisphere of the cortex, are composed of several different talents of mind, and their neural proximity may indicate psychological similarity. There are probably specific and separate control systems for weight, hunger, and rage, for decoding spoken language and producing it, for memory for riding a bicycle, and thousands more. This means there are many different divisions of the small minds, including memories, thought, and perception.

There is physiological evidence for different sorts of memory, which have different neural mechanisms. One kind is the limited store of verbal facts and information that is educated and tested; another is our complex and varied representation of the world. This representation memory probably contains the vast bulk of ordinary knowledge, and I am sure that it does not operate like a simple "information-processing" system. There are too many kinds of memory in too many separate parts of the mind for this to be true — memories of faces, locations, smells, movements, sights. Verbal memory may work like a simple machine, but not the other kinds.

There is certainly a change within us after our experiences. Suppose a man attacks us in a street; we won't go there very often. If the food at a certain restaurant gives us pleasure, we return there again. The neatly structured, single-minded view of this change is that another small bit of memory has been altered, a supposed process somewhat like storing something specific in your word processor or in the memory bank of your calculator. This viewpoint is archaic, for it ascribes a kind of point-to-point representation to memory, as if everything we remember must somehow mirror something outside. But we are not computers, we are not possessed of a single kind of knowledge or remembrance. The changes within are not really like those of our machines.

In most cases, our mind's changes are like those of muscles growing stronger with effort or of glands secreting more when exercise begins. Your abdominals may become stronger after working out, but it would be archaic to hold that these changed muscles "remember" the exercise; they are altered and work differently with experience.

Most likely there are different kinds of learning and knowledge that coexist within the mind. For instance, it is usually assumed that once a person has learned something he knows it. But the multimind view would ask, "Where is the knowledge in the mind?" Something learned in one small mind doesn't mean that it is learned throughout the mind. If we are looking for new learning, be it at school, in new political ideas, or even in psychotherapy, we should recognize that it is not always a matter of developing new abilities or skills.

Often it is more a matter of using that ability ("Wheeling in" the right small mind) at a given time. Many writers find they can't write a book while gaily writing other things all the time. One well-known writing instructor confided to me that she tells these people to write their books the way they do their letters.

Most people would agree that there are many different

mental talents and abilities. Many of the older views in psychology assume that there are many different general processes like perception, learning, and memory, all serving a single mind. I think this kind of understanding is beginning to have outlived its usefulness.

There is little reason to think that perceiving and remembering are in any way different; there is probably no reason to believe in the idea of memory as a specific component of mind anymore. Our remembrances — be they words said to us, exciting events like our marriage, general knowledge like knowing where Indonesia is — are probably spread throughout different multiminds. These older "faculties" of mind, like perception, memory, and thought, are probably useful mainly as chapter headings rather than as real and discrete abilities.

Similarly, the lack of success of current "computer simulation of cognitive processes" and of artificial intelligence programs is most likely due to the extremely oversimplified view of the mind to be modeled. I think setting up a machine that has quite separate routines — for body control, space, smell, and the other talents that move in and out of control with differing priorities — might have a better chance. Indeed, the trend in computers anyway is toward "multiprocessing," many different central processors joined together. What we need is more knowledge of the brain and mind to infuse into these programs. We already have the right operating system, as described herein.

I do not wish to say that the concept of a multimind itself is without its own particular difficulties. Multimind is a view that could justifiably be termed neophrenology, in that it considers many separate faculties of the mind. It has within it the same danger that the phrenologists eventually ran into. Their real problem was not their identification of the specific bumps on the head with mental abilities. That inevitably gave phrenology its bad name, but it could easily have been rectified. In fact, we are here drawing from evidence about similar patches in the brain.

The real difficulty with this kind of viewpoint is that one could go on forever, dividing and postulating mental talents, abilities, and other components of the mind. One critic might feel that I have slighted music; another might ask about whether mathematics is a talent or a lower-level and later ability, since it has little or no basic survival value and it must be trained. Other questions would concern the ability to think — then what about drafting, cookery, and the like?

It is for this reason that I am restricting the talents description to very large and probably innate centers of action, for which there is ample evidence to make this judgment. I am sure that many other activities normally called talents involve the participation of the talents I describe. Some may involve a redefinition of certain casts of mind. Perhaps creativity is not general at all but is domain specific: a different function dependent upon the part of the mind that is active. It would not surprise me to find that the process and the products of creation may be very different in talking, moving, and mathematics. Maybe we should speak of major talents and minor ones or talents and abilities, though it is not necessary to do so now. Multimind is intended to open us to this way of looking at ourselves, not to answer all the possible questions. Not yet, anyway.

PART III

SMALL-MINDED POLICIES

The management had called a mass-meeting of all employees.

"My friends," said the managing director, "I have to announce that, as from a month hence, this factory is to go over to total automation."

There was a gasp from the whole audience.

"All processes will be carried out by machines. This will mean that the work is done better, more quickly and more profitably."

"What about us?" someone called out.

"There is no cause for alarm. You will be paid as usual, with annual increments. You will continue to have the same subsidized canteen and sports facilities. All you have to do is come in on Fridays to collect your pay."

Nasrudin, a union official, stood up.

"Not *every* Friday, I hope?"

— The Subtleties of the
Inimitable Mulla Nasrudin

CHAPTER SEVEN

From Water Temperature to Watergate

THE MULTIMIND MODEL leads to a different vision of the mind. In a sense, it assumes that the mind is a kind of bastard hybrid system; a collage comprising many fixed and innate routines, all of which serve the mental operating policies that stretch over millions of years, millions of organisms, and millions of situations.

The policies of mind can influence our thought and judgment over an extraordinary range, once the evidence from water temperature to Watergate is placed together. While these policies may originally have developed to save space in the small brain of the codfish, they are still around in us.

Remember the Henry Youngman riposte in which the comedian was asked: "How do you like your wife?" "Compared to what?" he responded.

Our standard of comparison constantly shifts internally as well. There is a standard psychological demonstration that you might try (or you can simply imagine it). You will need three bowls of water (or a damp but willing imagination). Place one hand in a bowl of quite hot water and the other hand in a bowl of quite cold water for a few minutes, or just place your hands under the hot and cold taps. Then put them in a bowl of lukewarm water. The hand that was in the hot water feels cold; the one from the cold water feels hot. The senses transmit comparative information: each hand compares its current lukewarm experience to the previous one. Even as you know what is being demonstrated, the feeling persists.

An outside air temperature of 50° feels warm in winter but cold in summer; a salary of $500 a week sounds enormous to a student and insults an executive. A 200-gram weight in a series ranging from 100 to 200 grams is experienced as heavy, while in a series from 200 to 500 grams it is experienced as light. A sportscaster may look enormous compared to the jockey he is interviewing, tiny when talking with the center of the basketball team.

Comparison seems to operate in both physiological and psychological terms. I once took a winter vacation in Hawaii and arrived in 65° weather. I looked out on the beach to see hundreds, maybe thousands, of tourists — from Minnesota, I found out — in bikinis. I had never seen so many bikinis in my life, stretched out as far as I could see. At the same time the beach workers, native Hawaiians all, were cleaning the beach. They were wearing sheepskin coats!

We often don't know what is happening to us because we judge our own state of mind and mood using the small mind of comparison.

For instance, it would seem to most of us that people who had the great luck to win a lottery would be happier over a long period than people who have not. However, lottery winners were no happier one year after winning than before they won, and they found considerably less pleasure in mundane events than those who had not won. Why? The lottery winners may have adapted to their new fortune, thus shifting their comparison level. Instead of being delirious that they can afford a new car, they begin to complain about the standard of service at the Jaguar dealership.

Because our mind is really a coalition made up of competing entities, we do not always, even often, know what we think or believe. Part of us, probably somewhere in the self part of the brain, constantly tries to compare and sort out our own thoughts and beliefs.

When the different pieces of the mind are not in harmony, a condition called cognitive dissonance results. Since we compare the different aspects of the mind to each other, we try to reduce the dissonance. This continual comparison and adjudication helps explain why we behave in such puzzling ways. For instance, if we are asked to say something in favor of a cause, we will almost automatically come to believe more strongly in that cause. This is why companies often sponsor contests in which the participants are asked to dwell on the product. It may involve writing an essay in which they say why they like the product or thinking up new uses for the product. Cooking contests are a good example. The customer's involvement enhances the value of the product in his mind.

How does this happen? Consider these statements: (1) I know cigarette smoking causes cancer; (2) I smoke. Rational people would be uncomfortable trying to live with this contradiction. They can solve the problem in several ways: giving up smoking; consider cancer not such a bad thing; assume that a cure will be found by the time they get the disease; or, in the extreme, simply ignore the evidence. (The author of this theory, the social psychologist Leon Festinger, suggested that people can give up reading!)

Dissonance can be reduced by changing one of the ideas

so that it is no longer inconsistent or by attempting to reduce the importance of one of the ideas. For example, you can decide you really do not like the person you insulted or that what you said was a joke, not an insult. Dissonance can also be reduced by adding other ideas that are consistent with one of the beliefs. You could compensate for the insult by doing something especially nice for the person you slighted.

In one well-known study, sixty undergraduates were randomly assigned to one of three experimental conditions. Each student was first asked to perform a dull, repetitive task — placing twelve spools in a tray, emptying the tray, placing the spools in the tray, emptying it, and so forth — for one hour. Afterward, one third of the students were paid $1 and asked to tell a waiting subject (who was in cahoots with the experimenters) that the task was enjoyable and interesting. Another third of them were paid $20 to say the same thing. The final group, the control group, simply performed the task and was not asked to tell anyone how they liked the job.

All the students initially thought that the task was extremely dull. Later, they were asked to fill out a questionnaire unrelated to the purpose of the experiment and to rate how much they had actually enjoyed the task.

If we try to keep things simple and consistent, we would expect that those people who were paid only $1 would experience dissonance and change their attitude about the task, while those who were paid $20 would not experience dissonance and would not change their attitude. The $1 payee's inferences would be: "I wouldn't lie about such a silly thing for $1, so I must have really enjoyed it." Those paid $20 would think: "Hell, for $20 it's no skin off my back to lie about such an insignificant thing." The $20 would give them a valid reason for the inconsistency.

The results confirmed this prediction. When asked afterward by someone other than the experimenter to tell their true attitude toward the task, those paid $1 evaluated the task as significantly more enjoyable than did those paid $20 and the control group.

The inconsistency between these people's behavior and their initial attitude produced an uncomfortable state that prompted them to compare their attitudes and behaviors, then change the attitude so that it was now consistent with the behavior.

That is why something like signing an innocuous petition in support of a good cause, no matter what, will make you more likely to support the next good cause, because you now think more strongly of yourself as a supporter of good causes. Don't you know people who seem to live only for almost any good cause? A teacher whose income is far less than that of a friend who is a banker may decide that making money is "selling out." A starving artist claims that successful artists aren't pure. It also means that the fewer inducements you provide, the more likely you are to create attitude change. For instance, chronically underpaid workers, such as nurses, teachers, and social workers, often speak of the "psychic income" of their jobs.

Our tendency to be affected by the level of comparison is taken advantage of by salespeople and advertisers. Suppose a couple goes to buy a car. They are considering two: one for $7,000 and another $9,000. The $2,000 difference is important; they compare the cars carefully. The salesperson then shows them a $20,000 car, pointing out the features that are similar to those in the $9,000 car. When the couple gets back to deciding between the two cars they are considering, the $9,000 car begins to seem like a better deal, even cheap, in comparison.

These tendencies are well known among salespeople who

are often the best teachers of psychology in these situations because, unlike in academic thought, there is a real bottom line to their actions. For instance, you would think that if you are going to sell a $350 suit and a $55 sweater, you would be better off selling the sweater first. But a good salesperson will sell the $350 suit first so that the $55 sweater does not seem so expensive.

Companies often introduce a very expensive product, such as a $3,500 gold watch or a "designer limited edition" of a car, at a wildly inflated price. The price seems ridiculous, and one can hardly imagine paying a premium of $7,500 to get a status name on a car or double that for a special body design. But these premium items do more than sell themselves, they make the other products on sale seem less expensive.

Here is an extract from *Sales Management Magazine* as it was reprinted by *Consumer Reports:*

> If you were a billiard-table dealer, which would you advertise — the $329 model or the $3,000 model? The chances are you would promote the low-priced item and hope to trade the customer up when he comes to buy. But G. Warren Kelley, new business promotion manager at Brunswick, says you would be wrong . . . To prove his point, Kelley has actual sales figures from a representative store . . . During the first week, customers were shown the low end of the line . . . and then encouraged to consider more expensive models — the traditional trading-up approach . . . The average table sale that week was $550 . . . However, during the second week, customers . . . were led instantly to a $3,000 table, regardless of what they wanted to see . . . and then allowed to shop the rest of the line, in declining order of price and quality. The result of selling down was an average sale of over $1,000.

So we are quite easily fooled by a simple strategy involving a change in the comparison level. But, you say, this wouldn't happen in something important. Well, if you ask one group of physicians if they would use a new treatment if there is a 50 percent chance people will die using it, about 35 percent will say yes. If you ask another group if they would use it if there is a 50 percent chance people will be saved using it, 70 percent say yes. Of course both situations are exactly the same, and of course no physicians would have believed that they were so easily manipulated. But these are the people who may be trained in technical matters but not in the separated nature of their process of judgment itself. Can we let this go on and allow our small minds to step in even in life-threatening matters?

We may apply changing standards of comparison to different situations at different times. What is enough money at one time is not enough at another. This has been called psychological accounting: we shift items into different accounts. Suppose you are going to a play and lose $10 on the way. Would you still pay $10 for a ticket? Most people say they would. Suppose you have bought your $10 ticket and lose it on the way. Would you pay for another ticket? Most people say no. The loss in both situations is exactly the same, but it is not the same in psychological terms. In the first case the loss is not applied to our ticket account; in the second, the account has been used up.

Would you drive twenty minutes to save $5? It depends upon comparison. If you need a toaster and a store close to you has it for $25 and another store twenty minutes away has it on sale for $20, would you drive? Most people say they would. Suppose you are going to buy a jacket at a nearby store for $165 and a store twenty minutes away has the same one for $160. Most people say they would not drive the extra miles. They are less likely to drive when the savings represent a smaller amount of the total. The savings are equal, but how they are compared is not.

The mind, then, is systematically biased in several ways,

ways that allow us to make short cuts in judgment which are usually helpful. We don't use all the information available to us in making judgments, in the same way that our senses do not use all the information available to them—it would take too long. We wheel in comparison, a piece of the mind that enables us to make fast judgments. Sometimes these specialized mental pieces do go awry, for comparison, a quite basic neural routine and a generally useful and important piece of the mind, was not "designed" to do well in complex social judgments. So we are much easier to influence than we would like to believe.*

We are especially easy to influence because we are always comparing our behavior to that of other people.

Imagine that you are alone in a room and hear someone cry for help from the next room. Would you help? Probably. Now, imagine that you are sitting with a few other people when you hear a cry for help. Would you go to help? Yes, again? No, probably: you are three times less likely to help if there are six people in the room than if you are alone. The group we are in has a profound effect on us, more than we would like to think. We obey the authority of groups; we compare our attitudes with those of the group; we make decisions we never would have made if we had been alone. We change our standards and conform to the group.

How do you know where you belong? You are old or young compared to someone else, smarter or funnier than someone else. We make many social judgments by comparing ourselves to a standard, a reference group. This standard may shift our comparisons. I was once on my neighborhood touch football team and was, I believed, a good quarterback. I could throw longer and better than

*See Tversky and Kahneman's work for more.

anyone I knew. Of course, I was a 49er fan, too. At the time, the quarterback of the 49ers was being pilloried in the press: he was too old, his arm was no good, and so on. I was as down on him as anyone, sure that he couldn't throw.

When he finally retired, he happened to live across the street from me, and an enterprising friend asked if he could join our team, which he did. You should have seen him throw! You don't realize until something like this happens how different your standards can be and how easily you can hold different ideas apart. There he was, washed up, I thought, but out here a sensational thrower, with me, in my mind a good passer, looking terrible.

We constantly interact with other people who belong to a variety of groups: large ones such as business, professional, political, or social groups; small ones such as family, friends, club, or team. A fundamental part of our lives is spent determining how we compare to the rest of the group, where we fit into it. How we stand is sometimes based on an objective comparison. You can easily determine if you are taller or heavier than someone else by a simple and objective physical measurement.

But most of the time there is no objective way to compare ourselves with others. Most social situations are complex; there is no defined scale to tell you whether your attitudes and behavior are normal in a particular group. So we operate by social comparison: we seek out other people and compare our attitudes or behaviors to theirs. However, not just anyone will do for comparison. We look to those we admire or who we believe are like us: most of us would not compare our political beliefs to those of a group of drunks (unless we aspire to inebriation).

A member of a crowd may tend to act with less inhibition than an individual alone. Similarly, residents of large cities seem more likely to indulge in vandalism than those who live in less urban areas. The psychologist Philip Zimbardo abandoned a car in New York City and a similar car in Palo Alto, California. In New York, the car was systematically looted and vandalized within ten minutes. Interestingly, this violence was not started by juvenile delinquents but a middle-class family, who methodically stripped the car of its valuable parts. In Palo Alto, the car stood untouched for a week except by one thoughtful pedestrian, who lowered the hood to prevent the engine from getting wet during a rainstorm.

The large environments seem to destroy the formation of a reference group that contains standards of good behavior. When we do not fit in the reference group, we often pay a heavy price: we might be disliked, rejected, or treated badly. When there are differences between our attitudes and the group's, there may be pressure to change attitudes, to conform to the group's standard or to a new situation. Our minds are so comparative and in such independent pieces that we have little idea how easy it is to be manipulated. We do not use all the information we could.

Sometimes the result is the hilarious manipulation of our desires and our money. In *Influence*, Cialdini describes how his cousin took advantage of the tendency to ignore important information to put himself through college, buying and selling cars, but with a psychological twist to it.

Richard wrote good ads but thought of something new.

He usually received an array of calls from potential buyers on Sunday morning. Each prospect who was interested enough to want to see the car was given an appointment time — *the same appointment time*. So, if six people were scheduled, they were all scheduled for, say, 2:00 that afternoon. This little device of simultaneous scheduling paved the way for competition for a limited resource. Typically, the first prospect to arrive would begin a studied examination of the car and would engage in standard car-buying behavior such as pointing out any blemishes or deficiencies and asking if the price were negotiable. The psychology of the situation changed radically, however, when the second buyer drove up. The availability of the car to the prospect became limited by the other. Often the earlier arrival, inadvertently stoking the sense of rivalry, would assert his right to primary consideration. "Just a minute, now, I was here first." If he didn't assert that right, Richard would do it for him. Addressing the second buyer, he would say, "Excuse me, but this other gentleman was here before you. So, can I ask you to wait on the other side of the driveway for a few minutes until he's finished looking at the car? Then, if he decides he doesn't want it or if he can't make up his mind, I'll show it to you." Richard claims it was possible to watch the agitation grow on the first buyer's face. His leisurely assessment of the car's pros and cons had suddenly become a now-or-never, limited-time-only rush to a decision over a contested resource. If he didn't decide for the car—at Richard's asking price—in the next few minutes, he might lose it for good to that . . . that . . . lurking newcomer over there. The second buyer would be equally agitated by the combination of rivalry and restricted availability. He would pace about the periphery of things, visibly straining to get at this suddenly desirable hunk of metal . . . [And] the trap snapped securely shut when the *third* 2:00 appointment arrived on the scene. According to Richard, stacked-up competition was usually too much for the first prospect to bear.

So Richard went through college, selling cars quickly and for a good price because he created a situation in which very little of the available information was brought into mind and in which the process of comparison called up yet another policy of the mind. A specialized small mind was automatically wheeled into place: "compete and win for scarce resources," it might be called. The lessons from these processes could easily save you a lot of money without your resorting to schemes as elaborate as Richard's. If you are ever buying a car, try to have someone call the seller before you do and offer him a very low price. Your offer will then look quite good. (Send half your savings to the writer of this book.)

So scarcity affects comparisons: if there are two cookies in a jar, you will think them tastier and more special than if there are ten. This is the "buy now, limited time offer" phenomenon. Idealistic students will deny that seeing a photograph of a car with a sexy girl draped over it can influence them, yet they rate the car as faster, more expensive, and more desirable with the "extra accessory." After all, why else would there be so many sexy bodies in ads?

But we think, or would like to think, with one of our minds that these "small-minded" phenomena would only occur in relatively trivial situations, like buying a car or judging how fast we can run. In fact, we consistently underestimate the degree to which we can be manipulated, in part because we do not understand that very different pieces of our mind may be making the decisions, pieces that are different from the cold, sober, rational estimator of how we will act.

Most people are sure they would not carry out an order they consider wrong. But are they right? No. Under the right circumstances, ordinary people's judgment will slide along a path greased by continuous comparisons, and they will comply with the commands of an authority figure even when the request is extreme and uncalled for and there is no threat of punishment. We conform because we compare ourselves to others around us: if they are "all doing it," so do we.

In Stanley Milgram's classic experiment on obedience to authority, men responded to a newspaper advertisement for "participants in a psychology experiment" at Yale University. When each man arrived, he was introduced to the experimenter and another subject, "the learner" (actually a confederate of the experimenter). The subjects were told that the experiment was "an investigation of the effects of punishment on learning."

The "teacher's" job was to administer an electric shock every time the learner made a mistake. The experimenter strapped the learner into a chair and attached electrodes to his wrist. The learner expressed concern about receiving shocks, stating that he had a heart condition. When he was wrong, the teacher read the correct answer aloud and punished him by electric shock. There were thirty shock levels, ranging from 15 volts (labeled Slight Shock) to 420 volts (labeled Danger: Severe Shock). The two final switches, for 435 and 450 volts, were simply labeled XXX. Each time the learner made a mistake, the teacher was to administer a shock one level higher (15 more volts) than the previous shock.

Unbeknownst to the subject (teacher), the learner had been instructed to make frequent mistakes and never actually received any shocks, but as the experiment progressed, the learner began to complain about the shocks, express concern about his heart condition, and beg to be released. After the teacher administered 300 volts, the learner began to pound the walls; after that, he no longer answered.

How much shock would you have given? Almost no one says he would give the maximum shock. The results are, well, shocking! Although the teachers knew that the learner had a heart condition and heard him beg to be released, 62.5 percent of them complied completely with the request and gave the maximum shock of 450 volts. Even more startling, only 22.5 percent gave less than 300 volts, and in one variation, no one gave less than 300 volts.

There are many dramatic instances — in war, in brainwashing — of the ease with which we can be manipulated. But the point is that we should not be surprised. We have very limited resources, mentally, and by cleverly switching the comparisons, our judgments change radically.

Our mental operating system is so limited at any one time that the small mind, operating by comparison only, finds it difficult to resist such pressures to conform even when the group is merely a random collection of strangers and there is no explicit request to comply.

In the classic study of Solomon Asch, a number of unsuspecting volunteers were solicited for a psychology experiment on visual perception. One real subject and six phonies looked at lines of varying length. They were asked to identify which line on the second board was the same length as the one on the first. They answered in turn, with the real subject responding last. Although all the confederates picked the same obviously incorrect line, although there was no overt demand for group unanimity, although common sense says it would be very easy to resist this pressure, 32 percent of the real subjects conformed to the group pressure and gave the wrong answer. The effect on the comparing mind of a random collection of strangers is considerable.

The rules that people in different groups conform to differ. If you look at photographs of people in different eras you notice something startling: they all dress alike. This comparison covers different societies at the same time as well. In Rome, you do as the Romans do. In a mobile culture like America today, multiple societies operate at once, with its own references and levels of comparison.

When you change your reference group, you change many things about yourself. Recent law school graduates who go to work in prestigious New York law firms may find they need an entire new wardrobe, a different one than lawyers in a small town in the Sierras. Several factors determine to what extent we conform.

People are most likely to conform when faced with unanimous group opinion. In the Asch experiment, conformity was 32 percent. If, however, there is even one person who does not go along, conformity drops dramatically, to about 8 percent; it does not even matter if the other dissenter's answer is wrong.

Another important factor is group size. If you are sitting with someone in a lecture who says that it is boring, you may or may not agree. If ten other people say it is boring, you may begin to agree with them. In the Asch experiment, there is only 2.8 percent conformity with just one other person in the room, 12.8 percent with two, and about 30 percent with four people. Conformity does not increase with groups over four. Apparently we only need a certain amount to make our comparison; once defined, further confirmation is a surplus.

The many groups we belong to give us several simultaneous "small-minded" comparisons, almost at once. You may be a mother, an executive, and a member of a film club, a diet group, a political discussion society, and various other groups all at once. Groups usually intensify experience both for better and for worse; they can make our opinions more extreme, make it less likely that we will help someone, encourage us to loaf instead of work, and turn a set of individuals into a mob.

One important factor in that change of opinion in groups is social comparison. People want to be thought of positively and will modify their opinions to become liked. In one experiment, when subjects were shown "sneak previews" of others' opinions, they changed their own opinions in the more extreme direction. Thus a snowball effect of opinion change is created.

Groups can take on a life of their own. In one study, the subjects were asked to enter a booth in which they sat alone and listened to a discussion by college students. Although the subject did not know it, the discussion was on tape. In the first part of the discussion, one of the students said he was an epileptic. During the discussion, the subject heard what clearly sounded like an epileptic seizure coming from the student.

In some cases, the person in the booth thought he was the only one listening to the discussion; in others, the person thought he was part of a group of three; in another, a group of six. The effects were, unfortunately, startling; 85 percent of those who believed that they were the only other listener tried to help the epileptic immediately by reporting it to the experimenter; 60 percent of those in a three-person group tried to help; and only 30 percent of those in six-person groups reported it. It is not the supposed apathy of others that stops us from helping, it is a group comparison: if we don't hear anyone in a large group helping, we don't, either, because "it must be all right." So people die on the street in cities with thousands of people passing by, all most likely believing that since no one is helping they know what they are doing.

Comparing our behavior to that of others helps us define a situation, For example, a subject sitting alone in a waiting room hears noises in the adjoining room — someone climbing on a chair to reach something — then he hears a crash and a woman moaning in pain. Of the subjects who were alone, 70 percent rushed to the woman's aid. When the same scenario was played out when two subjects were waiting, the figure dropped to 40 percent. Apparently each waited for the other to define the situation as an emergency. Indeed, it has been found that once a situation is so defined (that is, someone stops to help), others are more likely to stop and offer assistance.

It can go the other way as well, sometimes with devastating results. Philip Zimbardo experimentally changed the levels of comparison. He simulated a prison in the basement of the psychology building at Stanford University and randomly assigned male students to the roles of prisoner and guard. The police even cooperated by picking up the prisoners in squad cars, complete with siren. The prisoners were treated realistically. They were fingerprinted, stripped, "skin searched," and given demeaning uniforms — dresses, with no underclothing, intended to "emasculate" the prisoners. They also wore a chain locked around one ankle. The guards were also uniformed and were given handcuffs, cell and gate keys, and billy clubs, even though physical violence was prohibited. They were told to maintain law and order and to be stern with the prisoners.

Soon the experiment took an unsettling turn. Some of the guards identified with their roles and began to enjoy their power over the prisoners. The prisoners rebelled at first, but after the rebellion was put down, the guards became more aggressive and the prisoners became more passive. Five prisoners were released early because of their severe anxiety and rage reactions. The experiment had to be terminated after only six days, rather than the two weeks originally scheduled, due to the prisoners' distress.

The guards were disappointed with the early termination, for they had quickly grown to enjoy their power roles. Outside the experiment the guards were normal, nondestructive people, as measured by standard psychological tests, but their apparently complete power over the prisoners resulted in arrogant, aggressive, and cruel behavior. This being an experiment, the prisoners could have left. But they did not leave, so strong are the comparative processes of the MOS, even though they were made acutely uncomfortable.

Some rather pedantic academics have criticized this and other social psychology studies because they are not exactly *real* prisons or concentration camps (the Milgram study was stimulated by Nazi atrocities). But thousands of people die in circumstances similar to these experiments; under similar conditions of restricted comparisons and thought coercion, people are raped, beaten, and robbed by others who may be simply responding with a small mind to a set of circumstances and don't "really" take it seriously. Their actions, however, have a reality far beyond trivial academic quibbles. The ease with which our minds can be altered is quite frightening.

So, there is an overarching mental policy of comparison: it judges the amount of light you need in a room, the temperature of your hands following previous exposure, how you buy things, and whether you might torture or help someone. In other words, the same neural circuits that originally developed to judge temperature and brightness now preside over the life and death of us all. Our mental structure is based on primitive processes of judgment, processes appropriate to an era long gone. Now quite important judgments, such as decisions about nuclear strategies and political campaigns, also funnel through the ancient system, and they sometimes have almost uncalculable consequences.

They helped to bring down a U.S. president. There was a break-in at the head of the opposition party's headquarters which came to be known as Watergate, an elaborate plan to spy on and harass the opposition. It is hard to understand how an experienced group of politicians could have approved such a ridiculous and wasteful operation, one that would have yielded little in any case. The story has recently come out, and it is the same MOS policy of comparison that is in some way responsible for the wild misjudgments of people like John Mitchell, who had run the president's original election campaign and also served as attorney general.

You probably remember that the pivotal break-in was proposed by a somewhat unusual operator, a man named G. Gordon Liddy. But how did he sell such a useless and transparently stupid idea? By "wheeling in" comparison, the same kind as shown in the water temperature demonstration earlier.

Liddy followed the car and billiard table salesmen's strategy: start very high and then lower your demand until something that would at first seem outlandish or ridiculous now appears quite middling.

Liddy went to planning sessions of the aptly named CREEP, the Committee to Re-Elect the President. He began by proposing a completely outlandish program of embarrassing and then undermining the Democrats by hiring a brace of call girls first to compromise them and then to spy on them, using walkie-talkies and taping their confessions at the threat of blackmail. He also proposed selective kidnapings, break-ins at Democratic headquarters, and other "dirty tricks" throughout the year, culminating with the presentation of the confessions obtained by the prostitutes at the Democratic convention in Miami. This plan, which would have cost a million dollars, was rejected by John Mitchell and the others at CREEP as preposterous.

Liddy later halved the plan, eliminating the most offensive elements — no kidnaping, only a few whores. This plan, costing $500,000, was also rejected.

Finally, for only $250,000, Liddy proposed a simple and comparatively mild break-in at the office of Lawrence O'Brien, at the Democratic headquarters in the Watergate office building, to see if any incriminating material could be found. Jeb Magruder, one of the participants, writes: "After starting at the grandiose sum of $1 million, we thought that probably $250,000 would be an acceptable figure . . . We . . . signed off on it in the sense of saying 'Okay, let's give him a quarter of a million dollars and let's see what he can come up with.' " A quarter of a million looked small after the initial proposals, as did the simple break-in compared to the wild scheme. It brought down the government.

With a view less clouded by the pressures of the moment, Magruder later wrote: *If he had come to us at the outset and said 'I have a plan to burglarize and wiretap Larry O'Brien's office,' we might have rejected the idea out of hand. Instead he came to us with his elaborate call-girl/kidnapping/mugging/sabotage/wiretapping scheme . . . He had asked for the whole loaf when he was quite content to settle for half or even a quarter"* (italics added).

Of course, it is not only comparison policies that work this way; "What have you done for me lately" is responsible for many of our overreactions to information in the media, from how we buy things to the research funds we will authorize for AIDS and for investigating the effects of chemicals in the atmosphere, and more. I will consider some of these questions again as we return to the question of why people copy a suicide they hear about.

CHAPTER EIGHT

Piece of Mind 2: Consciousness and the Invisible Fast Paths Inside the Mind

WE WOULDN'T BE in all this trouble if the mind were somehow unlimited in its capacities. If we could sort simultaneously through many possible ways of judging, deciding, and thinking we probably could act more appropriately in many different situations: we might not treat sudden competition as an immediate sign of scarce resources, and we might not overreact to emergencies.

However, with a complete mental system it might take us fifty years to decide if something was really an emergency, and we might have a head so large that we couldn't run away, anyway. So we have a limited central system that wheels in these separated bits, at whim sometimes. That is the conscious part of the mind.

The central and pivotal point of the mental system's operation is consciousness. Countless stimuli reach us at any moment; some are filtered out by the senses; some are organized and simplified. We must select the most important ones at any one moment, those with the highest priority. These items may be real emergencies, such as a threat to safety. Some may be immediate concerns, such as "watch that car in the left lane; he's weaving all over the road." Some may be chronic concerns, such as earning enough money to support our family, and some may focus on any new events, such as a person entering the room.

Consciousness is, to use a metaphor, the "front page" of the mind. It is as changeable as the front page of a newspaper, as it reflects the different important events of the day. The "headlines" set priorities for action. The priority system gives events that affect survival, like pain or a need for food, fast access to or dominance of consciousness. Suppose you are having a discussion in which you maintain that our minds are not disturbed by anything except rational argument. Then, suddenly, you get a cinder in your eye. Suppose you have a toothache, or a need for elimination, or have your hand near a flame? Your "higher" concerns vanish immediately.

Consciousness is the top part of the mental operating system and is sensitive to transient changes in our circumstances, our food supply, inner states, external threats — its contents career from one urgency to another, from emergency to necessity, constantly noting any significant changes in the world. It embodies the policy of "Don't call me unless something new and exciting happens."

Since our needs constantly change, consciousness splits at times to handle multiple needs; it alters through the day, from full wakefulness to drowsiness, from active thought to the bizarre ideation of dreams. Our adjustment to the world is very tentative and delicate.

To define it (although no single definition will really do): consciousness is the awareness of awareness, according to John Dewey. I think that definition differentiates human consciousness in the main from that of other animals'. There may well be different forms of awareness and consciousness in different animals, and probably within our own brain as well. When we wheel in one of the components of mind we are not necessarily conscious that we are doing it; the process is somewhere in awareness.

But being aware that we are aware is superior to the automatic selection of small minds. It implies the faculty or talent of the self. To know that we are aware of something presupposes an idea of who we are. So, consciousness, in the multimind view, involves the participation of the talents of the governing self described earlier. It is the center of the mind wheels, the controlling and directing force.* It most likely involves the area of the brain which represents our idea of ourselves and which receives information from the many different talents and modules in the brain. It probably has a role in organizing and directing many of the small minds we call into play, those minds that are combinations of the talents and modules.

As we know, the mind is limited in its capacity; only a small portion of the small minds are active at any one moment. Therefore we need to know how things get "on" our mind; that is, how do certain things enter consciousness and what happens when they do? There is an enormous network of invisible fast paths in the mind which have evolved to simplify the task of judging and thinking. For the most part, these help in perceiving, remembering, thinking, and organizing the world, but we should be aware of them, for we are often fooled by the information that gets in, and it often can call up the wrong routine, like suicide.

Here I will show how many occurrences, such as strong emotions or unexpected, very recent, striking, or vivid events can enter consciousness along these fast paths. And, unbeknownst to us (or outside full consciousness), the small

*"The mind *wheels*" is, of course, intended both ways: that there are wheels in the mind and that the mind as a whole wheels.

minds that are wheeled in affect our perception and judgment. As the thirteenth-century Persian poet Jalaludin Rumi wrote: "What bread looks like depends upon whether you are hungry or not."

The normal strategies of the mental operating system—simplification, exclusion of information—make us continually overreact from the little information we finally do select and allow to enter consciousness. When the news reports a murder in a distant city, we tend to think of the world as a more murderous place. When someone famous comes down with breast cancer, it becomes a national concern. When you are frustrated in traffic, you can become frustrated about your progress at work or the state of your marriage as well.

Whatever enters consciousness is greatly overemphasized.

It does not matter how the information enters; it may get in from a television program, a newspaper story, a friend's comment, a strong emotional episode, or just something that is easily recalled—all that gets in is overemphasized. We ignore more important or more valid evidence that is available to us and focus on what we already know.

Politicians have taken advantage of this in planning their campaigns. In primary elections, those who are astute enough to place all their resources on an early victory in small and unrepresentative places like New Hampshire often get the media attention and the consequent attention of the electorate: Jimmy Carter did it in 1976, and Gary Hart in 1984, by doing "better than expected."

We search for a simplifying pattern in our perceptions of the world. To be useful, our perceptions must adequately reflect the important events in the world around us. People approaching must be seen if we are to avoid bumping into them. We have to be able to identify food before we can eat it. But the sensory information is so chaotic and complex that a fundamental policy—number 4, "What is the meaning of this?"—is to organize things into a pattern even when there is none. We look up at a cloud and see shapes in it—a whale, a dagger. We can't go back, either. Once we learn a language we cannot hear it anymore as a collection of sounds. If we are familiar with flowers, we cannot fail to distinguish a buttercup from a dandelion.

But we are usually unaware of the MOS policies wheeling into action. We experience neither the individual stimuli nor rules of organization being applied. Rather, we almost literally draw conclusions about reality on the basis of the suggestions and cues brought in by the senses.

We are like paleontologists in that we "flesh out" living beings from the meager "bones" awarded us. Note how little information it takes for you to recognize someone: it may only be a flash of color of their arriving car, the sound of a chuckle in the distance, or even a hello on the phone, whose circuits transmit less than 10 percent of the tones in a voice. And then the person appears, instantly assembled from the pieces.

In order to act quickly, you assume much about the world you perceive. Suppose you are entering a room. You immediately assume it has four walls, a floor, a ceiling, and probably furniture. On entering a room, we do not inspect it to determine whether the walls are at right angles or that the room is still there when we leave it. If we constantly inspected everything in our environment, there would be no time to do anything. But we are oblivious to the assumptions inside our mind. And the situation is worse.

We are oblivious to the fact that our own opinions swing around wildly. We simply experience different opinions

at different moments and don't ever know that they are
in conflict. It takes a formal study to determine how and
under what conditions these opinions change.

One study took place, not in a laboratory, but in a shopping center. It investigated shifts in opinions when people
experienced a mild but pleasant surprise. In this case, the
surprise was trivial. On entering the shopping center some
people, the subjects, found a dollar bill—deliberately placed
by the experimenters.

About a half hour later these people were interviewed
by someone with no apparent connection to the dollar bill,
which was never, of course, mentioned. They were asked
seemingly neutral questions, such as: "How happy are you
with your marriage?" "How frequently does your car need
major repairs?" "Do you plan to buy the same make of
refrigerator again?"

Compared with people who did not find a dollar, those
who did had better marriages, less trouble with their cars,
and were more likely to get the same fridge again!

When we are in a given mood, such as anger, we are
more likely to recall other times when we were angry, and
the same is true about pleasant times. This is probably why
people worry if their boss "got up on the wrong side of
the bed" and why seemingly minor uplifts, like getting
flowers, can make the whole day go better. The boss's upset, although it had nothing to do with you, will make him
or her more likely to remember upsetting things about
your job performance than at other times.

The wisdom of the commonplace "Have a nice day"
takes on new significance: smiling creates an external feedback system that we know about; others will be more likely
to smile and a happier time will be had. However, the act
of smiling, of finding something nice, may well also create
the same kind of internal feedback system in which the

smile actually stimulates further good feelings. In essence, we watch ourselves smile. And then other happy moments in our memory are more accessible to the part of the mind that is operating in consciousness.

The unexpectedly strong effect of the pleasure of finding a dollar is just one indication that emotions are among the most important components of mind. A mood or a feeling can color an entire interchange, a day, or even an era. Lovers may mutually ignore their partners' many slights and oversights while in love, as do enemies during détente.

Feelings are a basic talent of the mind, more basic than most of us would like. They were here before we were. It is easy to recognize emotions as a separate part of the mind since they have an automatic and involuntary quality. We can't help getting angry at someone or falling for him or her; someone desirable may make us blush uncontrollably.

We can often feel the small minds swinging in and out quite easily as we "get emotional," causing a great stirring up in the body. In sports this is called pumped up and in psychology it is called arousal; in affairs of the heart it is called hot. The components of arousal, which include cardiac, vascular, hormonal, and neurotransmitter components, both prepare us for action and signal to the governing part of the mind that something important is happening. We are organized by our specific emotions to act, fight, fear, approach tenderly.

And we remember those times of strong emotion; the stirring up seems to be our own internal marker to the rest of the mind that something important is happening. All the people of my generation know exactly where we were when John F. Kennedy was murdered and exactly what happened to them just before and after the reports of the killing. It is as if the strong emotion fixes our memories of those moments, marking them for us.

And in all our lives there are similar moments that we will always remember: an announcement of marriage, the death of a loved one, unexpected shock. We can't do anything about it; we are primed by this component of mind.

But emotions also amplify our experiences. When in love, we can hardly think about anything else. When we are emotional about someone, it usually means that both our positive and negative feelings are unconsciously amplified, and we act badly toward those for whom we once had such hot love. This is why, I'm afraid, strong feelings of love often turn to hate once a relationship is over. That small mind containing the heightened feelings and the memories and the modular reactions is still in place, but the amplification is now focused on the rejection and disappointments.

Many people are aware that their emotions in some way color thought and that Freud and others have often pointed this out. But the multimind perspective is more radical: through it we can see that the much-prized and "higher-level" mental activities such as creative thought, judgment, language, and the like take place in the same wheeling routines as do simple emotional reactions. In all these operations, specific components of mind are wheeled in and out of consciousness as in a bewildering dance. So it is not surprising that philosophers, psychologists, and cognitive scientists are often confused about the nature of human thought.

On the one hand, we are certainly the most creative species that has ever lived. We have invented everything from agriculture to cities to space travel. On the other hand, we seem almost like idiots at times. We make the same dumb mistakes over and over again because of the independent "pieces of mind" that are often wheeled in without our conscious control. We hold nuclear weapons with the same hands designed to guide one spear and with a mental system designed to operate in a world populated by a few million people, not several billion. So we are almost inevitably "designed" to have the wrong reactions. Consider this situation:

> Let us suppose that you wish to buy a new car and have decided [on] either a Volvo or Saab . . . *Consumer Reports* informs you that the consensus of their experts is that the Volvo is mechanically superior, and the consensus of their readership is that the Volvo has the better repair record. Armed with this information, you decide to go and strike a bargain with the Volvo dealer before the week is over. In the interim, however, you go to a cocktail party where you announce this intention to an acquaintance. He reacts with disbelief and alarm: "A Volvo! You've got to be kidding. My brother-in-law had a Volvo. First, that fancy fuel injection computer thing went out. $250. Next he started having trouble with the rear end. Had to replace it. Then the transmission and the clutch. Finally he sold it in three years for junk."

How do you feel about the car now? Most likely you will strongly reconsider your decision to buy the Volvo. But think about it: the information you received only tells you that one more person out of thousands does not like the Volvo. The magazine may have surveyed tens of thousands. Though the brother-in-law is not an expert, you are strongly influenced by a single case.

Any information, when it gets into consciousness, can affect all current or subsequent experiences. When you are having an argument, even a trivial one about the color of your jacket or about whose turn it is to clean the kitchen, your opinion of almost everything, from your spouse's cooking to the chances for nuclear war, all be-

come much more dour. It happens because we are unaware of the piece of mind that is now in control, in this
case anger. The reactions are automatic, involuntary, and
the switching mechanism is outside the reach of our consciousness.

But this procedure of fast judgments — MOS policy 4:
"Get to the point!" — is a basic, important, and generally adaptive routine of the mind. It serves an important purpose: to put us on the alert to the most recent
information, even at the cost of ignoring past knowledge. If you are walking along a mountain trail and you
see someone ahead of you mauled by a wild animal, is
the generally safe record of the path of any value? No;
you get away quickly. The same rapid focus on recent
information can also help in the modern world when
conditions change.

Consider this: in the summer of 1980 a DC-10 crashed
in Chicago. On the day it crashed, what do you think
you would have done if you had been scheduled to fly
on a DC-10? You probably would have canceled your
reservation. Here our tendency to overgeneralize is
clearly adaptive: it protects against dangers due to
changing circumstances, in this case, the increasing wear
on the load-bearing struts in the wings of the DC-10s.
This kind of mental mechanism, combined with the
emergency reaction, may have gotten our ancestors out
of a lot of trouble: it allows us to adapt quickly to
changes that may well signal danger, but it makes mistakes in a stable situation.

Once we get anything in our mind, it is hard to get it
out again. This is why, unfortunately, we seem to need
disasters to keep our attention on specific events. It is
probably a consequence of our throwing away so much
information. The DC-10s were fixed. In Bhopal, the release of a lethal amount of toxic chemicals stimulated an

analysis of the degree to which such chemicals were already in the air around us in the United States and Western Europe. This was an analysis that should, and perhaps would, have been done sooner were it not for the way we are designed to receive information. The slow release of toxins stays out of mind because the changes are slight; then a disaster occurs, and all attention is fixed on it and similar problems. Then it is forgotten and we move on to the next problem.

Indeed, we can be influenced by ideas that we know are faulty, fallacious, or fanciful. And our beliefs persist even after they have been proved wrong.

In one study, people were asked to read information that was very damaging to a public figure. Their attitude toward the person was measured before and after they read the material. Afterward, of course, their attitude changed in a negative direction. Then they were told that the information they had just read was a mistake; it was not about that public figure at all and had been made up. Their attitudes were again assessed, and they were still more negative to the public figure than when the study began. And the change persisted for weeks!

I am sure this irrational persistence of a change in attitude is due to the wheeling in of a specific small mind that begins to make apparently sensible connections and ties up the evidence rather well. If the story was about the misuse of funds for a water project, the person might think, "Well, he probably misused public funds in that nuclear power scandal, too," and when the original impetus is removed — EXEC CLEARED IN WATER SCANDAL — the damage is done. Movie stars are probably wise in paying a lot to get good public relations agents.

All these phenomena point up the need for a new way to teach thinking, a way that recognizes that we have special mechanisms that are not good for judgment in the modern world. We ourselves are "flying without instruments," judging the operations of government, airplanes, medical interventions, without the benefit of training the part of us that can properly judge. We must learn to trust our personal judgments less than we do and become aware of the thought processes that come as standard equipment with our mental operating system.

Many pieces of the mind simplify and speed up thought. With these separate routines we classify information, categorize similar items, and use many different kinds of simplifying short cuts. Consider the immense number of colors we can see. We encounter more than 7,500,000 colors, but in most societies only eight color names are commonly used. It is simpler to call a tomato, a sunset, and an apple each red than to differentiate them by orangy red, luminescent red-orange with streaks of blue and black, and pure red speckled with green.

We can do all this, but it is unnecessary unless we are writing poetry or preparing to paint a picture. "Red" is enough for the simple purposes of daily life. Red and other major color names are examples of categories. Technically, a mental category is a MOS routine that selects and sorts items that can be considered equivalent. Some categories are universal, probably due to universals in the world. Color is a good example and is probably innate. The structure of the eye controls the categories most languages use for colors. The human visual system codes information in two ways: in black and white and in color combinations of red, yellow, green, and blue. In a study of almost a hundred languages, Berlin and Kay determined that color terms always appear in the following sequence:

```
white            green                 purple
black → red →    yellow → brown →      pink
                 blue                  orange
                                       gray
```

So if a language has only two color terms, they will always be black and white; if three, they will be black, white, and red; if there is a fourth, it will be either green, yellow, or blue. The fifth and sixth will be the two remaining of green, yellow, and blue. The next four will always be the four remaining colors in one order or another.

In addition to the basic natural categories, like color, there are artificial categories, which refer to the attributes of objects like chairs or buildings. It is easy to judge the best example of a natural category; it is harder with artificial categories. It is easier to judge whether something is "more red" than whether it is "more of a chair."

Some categories are peculiar to our culture. Is 15,000 lira a good price for shoes? How much is that, the American tourist asks, in "real money"? When the weather report says it will be 28° Celsius, most of us have to translate that figure to know if it will be hot or cold.

Categories are arranged around a core of best examples or prototypes that most typify the category: a man in a limousine with a telephone is a typical tycoon; a love of wine is typically French. A typical example may not always be the one we meet most frequently. For instance, which bird do you think is mentioned most often in written English? Most people think it is the robin. A robin flies, has feathers, tugs at worms, makes a nest, sings, announces the arrival of spring — all quite birdlike. However, the bird that is most often mentioned is the chicken. The chicken is not unfamiliar, but it does not typify our concept of bird. We are more likely to put chicken in the category of food than bird. We think a robin is more of a bird than a chicken. The sentence "A robin is a bird" is recognized more quickly than "A chicken is a bird." In another study, Eleanor Rosch asked people to fill the blanks in this sentence—"____is virtually____"—with the numbers 100 and 103. There was a clear preference for "103 is virtually 100" over the reverse, "100 is virtually 103." Our preference for round numbers and multiples of 10 is an example of how our mental system needs simplicity and order.

After something enters the mind, several small minds decide whether it is worth knowing about: which facts go into cold storage and which are placed on the fast path into consciousness. These short cuts are simplifying strategies that we use to make judgments and solve problems. There is a tradeoff in their use: we may sacrifice accuracy for speed. In life, we must usually rely on incomplete information to make judgments, reason, and solve problems. We need these several mental rules of thumb to yield an immediate guide to decisions.

Representativeness is the judgment that an object is typical of its category. A robin, for instance, is quickly judged to be a bird; it is representative of birds. A chicken is less so. A thin, precise man is often thought representative of computer programmers. This short cut involves matching prototypes.

However, using representativeness as a short cut can lead to the mistake of overgeneralization. For instance, we often tend to judge concrete or vivid examples of a category as representative when they are not. Something that is striking or something we see or hear at first hand overpowers other, more remote evidence, like that in a newspaper.

When there was a nearly catastrophic accident at the Three Mile Island nuclear reactor in 1979, its effect in influencing people to protest against the use of nuclear power was dramatic. The accident was judged to be representative of nuclear power plants, and it overwhelmed entirely the generally good safety records of these plants (whatever one may think about nuclear power).

A single case has a striking influence on us due to the multiple judges within; statistics can be easily ignored. At the beginning of a movie or novel, therefore, a disclaimer may appear that warns against the overuse of representativeness: "Any resemblance to persons living or dead is purely coincidental."

Another of the fast tracks into consciousness is the availability of information, the ease with which relevant instances come to mind. Events that are considered important or that occur more frequently are more easily retrieved from memory. One can see immediately that our memories have to be quite limited; of all the events you experienced last summer, how many do you remember?

The problems that a "perfect memory" would cause were well described by Borges in his story "Funes the Memorius":

> We, at one glance, can perceive three glasses on a table; Funes, all the leaves and tendrils of fruit that make up a grape vine. He knew by heart the forms of the southern clouds at dawn on the 30th of April, 1882, and could compare them in his memory with the mottled streaks on a book in Spanish binding he had only seen once and with the outlines of the foam raised by an oar in the Río Negro the night before the Quebracho uprising. These memories were not simple ones; each visual image was linked to muscular sensations, thermal sensations, etc. He could reconstruct all his dreams, all his half-dreams. Two or three

times he had reconstructed a whole day; he never hesitated, but each reconstruction had required a whole day. He told me: "I alone have more memories than all mankind has probably had since the world has been the world." And again: "My dreams are like you people's waking hours." And again, toward dawn: "My memory, sir, is like a garbage heap." A circle drawn on a blackboard, a right triangle, a lozenge — all these are forms we can fully and intuitively grasp; Ireneo could do the same with the stormy mane of a pony, with the herd of cattle on a hill, with the changing fire and its innumerable ashes, with the many faces of a dead man throughout a long wake. I don't know how many stars he could see in the sky.

Because of his extraordinary memory, it took Funes the same amount of time to recall events as the events themselves took: an entire day to remember an entire day. As a result, Funes forfeited the future. In ordinary life, we need to act quickly, and our mental system serves this need by retaining only a piece of the world, an easily available, simplified version of events.

A good example of how simple our version is can be found analyzing the answers to a basic question: What day is it? If our minds were in some way representative of the world there should be no difference, but this is not the case. On a weekday it takes longer to answer this question than it does on a weekend, and Wednesday takes the longest to remember. This probably happens because we judge days by their proximity to the weekend.

In fact, we are so small-minded and oversimplified that most of the time we cannot even remember things we see every day. Can you quickly say which letters are on the "7" of the phone dial? Most people cannot. Can you tell which of these depicts the real penny? And try this: say the months in order, time yourself, and count the mis-

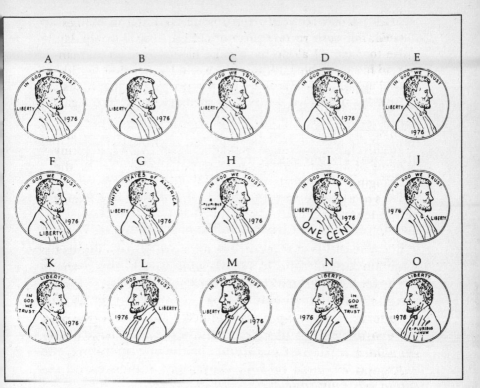

Which Drawing Is Accurate?

takes. If you are like most people, you did it well. Then try and recite the months of the year backward and time yourself. It probably took longer, and you most likely made few, if any, mistakes. Then try to name the months of the year in alphabetical order. It is surprisingly difficult, especially considering that you know the months—and have just repeated them twice—and you know alphabetical order. It is difficult because our mental system is designed to do only a few things well, and not much else.

Our memory is perhaps the ultimate in selectivity, and

when we select something in memory, it often brings up those other selections that were "laid down" at the same time.

The other night a friend put on a record that was popular when I was in graduate school. I hadn't listened to it for fifteen years, and as soon as I heard the first note I had a strange experience. I recognized the whole song immediately, but I also experienced a whole period of my life again. I could smell once again the orchard I lived in. I could almost see the faces of friends not seen (or even thought of) in fifteen years. There was my old blue '56 Chevy convertible. It had a top that never worked, I remembered. I often drove it to the beach at night. When I heard that song, I could once again smell the night air, see the sky, and feel the car slipping around the winding curves of the road out to the beach.

The same kinds of simplifying rules work in recall. Our memory operates like a storehouse, using and overusing those items on the fast path. In a sense, it is easy to understand why this system should be the one operating: the things we use a lot take priority; they influence and organize our experiences.

In one experiment, people were asked first to name any fruit that begins with the letter a, then a fruit beginning with p. The second question was answered faster. The first question presumably summoned up all the relevant information about fruits and their names, making the second question more easily answered.

You can see why this system would be functional. Like other mental short cuts, it would enable us to have access to many different kinds of information at different times, each package of information associated with different contingencies.

When I recently went back to a small hotel I had previously visited in London, I was surprised to find out that I somehow knew how to turn, on an unfamiliar street, to find the telephone box. For years I was unaware that I remembered this piece of information. But I had access to it only when I was in London. We can keep a few simple pieces of the world in mind, and for the most part we get on perfectly well.

However, the use of this piece of mind—availability—can lead to errors in judgment and in our world view. People who are out of work and thus spend a lot of time at the unemployment office, where they meet others who are unemployed, overgeneralize and overestimate the rate of unemployment. Hometown fans often overestimate how good their team is, as do chauvinists. Someone actually said to me once, "Haven't you noticed how many great Bulgarian authors there are?"

We use these short cuts to make fast judgments, and they probably result in more efficient judgments, but they also lead to systematic biases. When people are asked to judge the relative frequency of different causes of death, they overestimate the frequency of well-publicized causes, like homicide, tornadoes, and cancer, and underestimate that of less remarkable causes, like diabetes, asthma, and emphysema. So decisions are made to fund research on why people murder, and little on the constant crises like diabetes. It is easy to get money for disaster victims, not so for asthma sufferers.

Two psychologists, Amos Tversky and Danny Kahneman, read groups of students lists of well-known people of both sexes. In each list, the people of one sex were more famous than those of the other. When the students were asked to estimate the proportion of men and women on the lists, they overestimated the proportion for the sex with more famous people on the list. That is, if the list contained very famous women (such as Elizabeth Taylor) and only moderately well known men (such as Alan Ladd), then subjects overestimated the proportion of women on the list. Their judgments were biased by the ease of recall of specific examples.

One particularly important consequence of the way the mental operating system uses short cuts is that vivid information gets on the fast path and becomes very influential in judgment, as noted for the man who was thinking of buying a Volvo. Since television makes information so available to millions, any situation it portrays is amplified. There have been many instances of violence, some of it quite brutal, which were imitated from television. Television is a violent place, and its programs exaggerate the amount of crime in society. The viewing of so much crime has an effect: people who watch television a great deal perceive society as more violent than people who watch it a little. And adults as well as children appear to learn violent behavior from television.

The wide television exposure of the first airplane hijacking in the United States was followed by a large number of hijackings in only a few years. After viewing a murder in which ground glass had been used, a child was found putting ground glass in his parents' dinner to see if it would work as well as it did on television. When the Tylenol laced with cyanide was given a lot of publicity, a series of other food tamperings and poisonings followed. Even Halloween candy was doctored. That year parents came to my door with their children and looked carefully at the candies I gave them — all because of one person in Chicago who inserted some poison in a few jars of Tylenol.

The airing of the program *The Doomsday Flight*, which involved a bomb threat to an airliner, was followed by twelve bomb threats to airlines within a week — an 800 percent increase from the previous month. When the show appeared in Australia, one airliner was threatened with a bomb.

The exact imitation of something on television is comparatively rare. However, the continuous observation of aggressive actions on television can lead to more generalized aggressiveness. The television watchers are more likely to switch into violence; adults who view a lot of violent television have a lower physiological response to violent scenes than those who watch less violence.

The medium of television itself cannot be directly blamed for violent behavior. Television programming responds to demand: programs with aggression and violence are popular. However, there have been many studies and reports of the effect of these programs on violence, and the relationship of televised violence to social violence is clear: televised violence gets into the fast path of the mind and violent behavior does increase.

The publicity given to suicide is a good example of how vivid information can have extreme and unforeseen effects, due to the tendency of the multimind to respond to vivid information in consciousness. Suicides of prominent people are often reported on the front page of the newspaper. And immediately after a highly publicized suicide, the number of suicides increase in the same way that violence does. We are not surprised, at this point. But there is a great increase in accidents, commercial airline crashes, and automobile fatalities, too.

How does this happen?

The accidents do not increase throughout the country, so it is not a general phenomenon. They increase only where the suicide has been given wide publicity. Is it bereavement? Do the publicized deaths throw people into sadness and thus cause deaths in sympathy? No, because the stories of single-person suicides seem to stimulate single-person deaths only, and stories of multiple deaths, due to suicide or combined suicide and murder, cause similar later deaths.*

Hearing about a suicide is thus quite contagious: every publicized suicide stimulates fifty-eight more "copycat" suicides. The more space given to a suicide story in the media, the more subsequent suicides. Research by the sociologist David Phillips of the University of California has expanded what has come to be known as the Werther effect. (If I had registered what was happening with Marilyn Monroe, I might have been the author of the Ornstein/Monroe effect.)

The Werther effect is not named (as is usual) after an academic investigator but after Goethe's hero Werther, who committed suicide in *The Sorrows of Young Werther,* an eighteenth-century novel that immediately became popular in Europe and stimulated suicides in every country in which it was read. It caused such devastating reactions that the book was banned for a time in France.

More chilling than the copycat suicides are the dramatic increases in airplane crashes and auto accidents. Phillips points out that these surplus "accidents and disasters" are probably suicides, but done in a way so as to conceal the intent. People often don't wish it known that they have killed themselves, so they may simply drive off the road in a dangerous area, or a pilot may crash his plane in an area he knows to be particularly hazardous, a place quite likely to kill him.

Phillips reasoned quite brilliantly that the copying phenomenon would mean that the crashes of commercial air-

*In this analysis, I am again drawing from the excellent exposition by Cialdini in *Influence.*

liners within a few days of a publicized suicide would be more lethal than usual. The driver of a car could decide to go off the road at high speed, a pilot could swerve into another plane, and so on. Phillips presents convincing evidence that the fatalities are three times greater in these crashes than the norm, indicating that there probably is a deliberate element in them.

It is hard to believe that we would have to be careful when scheduled to fly from a city in which there has been a recently publicized suicide or that the effect of the suicide could be felt by someone driving on the freeway, but such is the complicated effect of our multiple mind and its priorities.

We are built to respond simply and quickly. Our judgment process operates by a set of fast paths; we build internal categories to simplify our perception and judgments based on a network of invisible structures. We are primed to respond to what's on at the moment and sometimes we overreact. We are primed by emotions to alertness or action to avoid emergencies.

And it is on the level of priorities that social factors probably have great influence on MOS processes. With great effort, people *can* decide to forgo many normal sensory needs, as in religious systems, and emphasize others (this takes less effort), as in more hedonistic cultures. There is a continuum of control possible, from the man who will starve to death for his country (against practically everything in his mind and consciousness) to the one who will be "automatically" compelled to respond to every emergency. Surely the idea of conscious development would allow the choice of multiple actions and multiple ways of looking at a situation.

Anything that is given wide publicity in the media, such as the events with which I began this book, get fast reactions while constant problems get ignored. People die every day from improperly maintained cars and the constant pollution of factories, but when one factory explodes it causes a major response. We are not designed to look at things equably and statistically but immediately and personally. We don't buy the Volvo, and other, more important decisions involving the lives and deaths of others wheel around. We remain unaware because we do not understand the complexity within ourselves. We are prone to many tragedies because of the overapplication of the policies of the mind. But other tragedies exist within ourselves due to a lack of communication within the separated components of the mind. That and the problems of knowing others is the subject of the next section.

PART IV

KNOWING ONESELF
AND OTHERS

CHAPTER NINE

Piece of Mind 3:
Some Cases of the Crowd Within

SO FAR we have drawn evidence from several sources: brain physiology, cognitive and social psychology, studies of thinking and judgment. Now I wish to present evidence from extraordinary studies of hypnosis, of individuals in whom the talents of the self are lacking. These lay bare the diversity within, although in an exaggerated way.

That we are consistent and single-minded is a built-in delusion. It has resulted in many professional misjudgments about assessing, testing, and teaching people. And there are the associated delusions that have personal rather than political consequences. We judge each other harshly and often unfairly. We do not credit that other people are more complex than they may seem to our small-minded view of them. Marriages break up because of this delusion, employees do not work well, and we needlessly separate ourselves from the talents offered by others. We ignore many of the talents we might possess as well; our minds are capable of much more than we might ever have imagined.

Here we look further into a few cases of how the mind is divided, but the divisions are revealed on a higher level than the simple comparing processes of the senses or the fast paths of judgment. We consider several different kinds of phenomena — an interesting experiment in cognitive psychology, evidence from extraordinary procedures like hypnosis — as well as some recently studied spectacular "natural" experiments, clinical cases in which a subject is lacking a normal component of mind. Abnormalities develop or, even worse, the separate pieces of the mind rise to the surface, ungoverned. Here we look at some of the phenomena of dissociation, then a case where the normal feeling component is lacking, and finally a case where the normally coordinated and separate small minds lack any overall control, yielding the condition of multiple personality.

Have you ever looked at a dressing room mirror? At one moment you look full face at one image; then, all of a sudden, when you turn you suddenly see the same image, yourself, chopped up into several bits. This is what happens to the MOS when it divides and when consciousness becomes dissociated: some experiences can only be recovered under specific conditions.

In an early recorded case of hypnotically induced dissociation, Pierre Janet, a nineteenth-century psychiatrist, suggested to one of his patients under hypnosis that she would at a later time write letters to certain people, when she was out of the hypnotic state. She wrote the letters, but when shown them she had no recollection of having written them and accused Janet of forging her signature. She could not retrieve the information given her in another state of mind.

It happens to us all. Have you ever felt "out of it" and just snapped back, with no recollection of the time, as if you had just lost a half hour? You might have awakened after a night of drinking and asked, "Did I really do, or say, that?"

Some hypnotic investigations of the mind reveal the split levels of observation that coexist at the different centers of the mind. Two hundred years ago, Franz Anton Mesmer claimed he had discovered the property of animal magnetism, a new force of nature through which he could control and influence another person's experience. As a result, miraculous healing cures abounded. This was the beginning of the Western discovery of hypnosis.

Hypnosis is a way to dissociate the segments of the mind by yielding aspects of the governing self to others. Through a number of different inductions, the hypnotist engages and retrieves command of aspects of an individual's consciousness. People under hypnosis have been able to recall events otherwise inaccessible to their waking mind and have also been able to withstand extreme pain.

Perhaps the most relevant of the many phenomena of hypnosis, from stagecraft to magic, from the retrieval of memories to bizarre actions, is the technique of the hidden observer. Ernest Hilgard, of Stanford University, has used this technique to show that experiences "hidden" below consciousness may enter consciousness through hypnosis, when the normal barriers are down.

Hilgard hypnotized a man and gave him the suggestion that he would be completely deaf at the count of three. He then banged two wooden blocks next to the man's ear. The man did not react to the sound. Hilgard then said, "Although you are hypnotically deaf, perhaps some part of you is hearing my voice and processing this information. If there is, I should like the index finger of your right hand to rise as a sign that this is the case." To Hilgard's amazement, the finger rose.

Many different splits have been demonstrated under hypnosis; they show that the person can then attain control of something usually blocked to a portion of his mind. On command warts have been removed and migraine headaches relieved; people have stopped smoking and have forgotten traumatic episodes in their life. These splits can vary in strength, and when such splits become extreme or a permanent condition, a multiple personality may result, in which two or more minds coexist.

That several minds can coexist and cooperate has been shown in an ingenious cognitive experiment. In simple laboratory situations, an extension or division of consciousness can be learned and can be beneficial. It is commonly believed that you cannot perform consciously two complex operations at once: if two such activities are attempted at the same time, one will suffer somehow. Normally, when we do two things at the same time, at least one is already well learned; we sing an old song while following a new recipe. When this happens, the learned task is performed automatically and is below consciousness.

One study used two students, Diane and John, to see if people could learn to read and write simultaneously. They read short stories while copying a list of words that was rapidly being dictated to them. At first Diane and John found the task impossible. They read slowly and did poorly when tested later for comprehension. But after six weeks of training, they could perform both tasks easily and well.

Then the experiment became more difficult: Diane and John were required to write down whole sentences rather than words. Within weeks, they could simultaneously write about one subject while reading another at normal speed and with normal comprehension. So we learn that through training, the capacity of consciousness may be greater than we have assumed.

In some extreme situations, we can observe that the mind breaks up into the normally separate pieces within. This does not happen often. It usually occurs in childhood when the person's parents are violent and sadistic and extremely inconsistent: one day they may be sweet and solicitous, the next day they may beat or assault the child. Often there are almost unspeakable sexual assaults followed by aloofness. The child simply cannot understand what is happening and does not know how to think, how to act, and what to do.

For those who cannot bear the pain, there is a breakdown in the governing portion of the mind, and the apparent solution is to give full and independent voice to those multiminds. Then distinct personalities emerge: sometimes there are two, each one unaware of the other, which may help in avoiding conscious recognition of the pain and horror of their life. Sometimes two personalities coexist, and later a third one emerges, one that has all the memories of the independent first two. Sometimes several different "persons" emerge to handle the pain and the aggression. It is quite confusing to others.

I regard multiple personalities as important demonstrations, at least, of the multimind view. The idea that "we are all multiple personalities" is not true. We have a multiplicity of abilities and talents, but we are not potential multiples any more than we are potential schizophrenics. However, the study of multiples shows, in an exaggerated manner, the underlying diverse structure. They represent a great challenge to scientists, as EEGs from multiples look like the EEGs of different people, so we might learn much from them about how a personality is represented in the brain. But usually multiples need treatment.

I began this book with an interview with a man named Billy Milligan, who had committed several rapes and was later found to have committed other crimes. He was acquitted on the grounds that the person committing the crime was not himself but was *in* him. It was a startling verdict, but an important one, I think. He was later treated and seems to still be well. I do not wish to go into the ethics of the case here, but I do wish to present another interview with Milligan, for it reveals much about the fight for control and the splitting of functions in the mind—in this case, of course, in the extreme.

After Milligan was arrested, his lawyers spoke to him in the interview described earlier. They then decided to call in the public defender to show him the man's condition. They met not Billy but Danny, a frightened, traumatized boy. Then they asked to see "Tommy," an explosives expert. Danny withdrew.

> Milligan's body seemed to withdraw into itself. His face paled, eyes glazed as if turning inward. His lips moved as he talked to himself and the intense concentration pervaded the small room. [Private Detective] Schweickart's smirk faded as he held his own breath. Milligan's eyes drifted from side to side. He glanced around, like someone wakened from a deep sleep, and put his hand to his right cheek as if to feel its solidity. Then he leaned back arrogantly in his chair and glared at the two attorneys.
>
> Gary [Schweickart] let out his breath. He was impressed. "Are you Tommy?" he asked.
>
> "Who wants to know?"
>
> "I'm your lawyer."
>
> "Not my lawyer."
>
> "I'm the one who's going to help Judy Stevenson keep that body you're wearing out of jail, whoever you are."
>
> "Shit. I don't need nobody to keep me out of anything. No jail in the world can hold me. I can bust out anytime I want to."
>
> Gary stared him down. "So you're the one who keeps

slipping out of the strait jacket. You must be Tommy."

He looked bored. "Yeah . . . yeah."

"Danny was telling us about that box of electronic stuff the police found in his apartment. He said it was yours."

"He always did have a big mouth."

"Where did you learn about electronics, Tommy?" Judy asked.

He shrugged. "On my own. From books. Ever since I can remember. I wanted to know how things worked."

"And the escape-artist stuff?" asked Judy.

"Arthur encouraged me on that. Someone was needed to get out of the ropes when one of us was tied up in the barn. I learned how to control my hand muscles and bones. Then I got interested in all kinds of locks and bolts."

Schweickart thought for a moment. "Are the guns yours, too?"

Tommy shook his head. "Ragen is the only one allowed to handle guns."

"Allowed, who does the allowing?" Judy asked.

"Well, that depends on where we are . . . Look, I'm tired of being pumped for information. That's Arthur's job, or Allen's. Ask one of them, okay? I'm leaving."

"Wait . . . [Then Arthur comes into consciousness.]

"You have to forgive Tommy," Arthur said coldly. "He is a rather antisocial youth. If he weren't so clever with electronic equipment and locks, I think I would have banished him long ago. But his are useful talents."

"What are your talents?" Gary asked.

Arthur waved his hand deprecatingly." I'm just an amateur. I dabble in biology and medicine."

"Gary was asking Tommy about the guns," Judy said. "It's a parole violation, you know." Arthur nodded. "The only one permitted to handle guns is Ragen, the keeper of rage. This is his specialty . . ."

"You say you've *spoken* to Ragen," Judy said. "How does

that work? Do you talk to each other out loud or in your head? Is it speech or thought?"

Arthur clasped his hands. "It happens both ways. Sometimes it's internal and in all probability no one else knows it's happening. At other times, usually when we're alone, it's definitely aloud. I imagine if someone were watching us, he or she would think we're quite mad."

Gary sat back, pulled out his handkerchief and wiped the perspiration from his brow. "Who's going to believe this?" [Italics added.]

The jury did. But what is perhaps even more interesting in this case is the way in which the control function, usually a part of the governing portion of the mind, is embodied in a single created person, Arthur, who controls the "spot," the emergence into the light of one or more of the separate "people."

Others inside Milligan have specific and quite limited roles, very much like the talents. Ragen is one, Tommy another. One whom we do not meet in this extract is David, the "keeper of the pain," as Arthur describes him, the empath. So there's one for feeling, one for control and governance, one for rage, and on and on. It is quite an instructive, if extreme, case. Other, less dramatic multiples show quite different but seemingly complete personalities. But Milligan shows all the components: the feeler, the creative protector, the fighter, and more. And he shows what happens when the skin over the whole cracks.

But I wouldn't take Milligan as the progenitor of the idea that the whole person shouldn't be imprisoned for the crime of just one of the parts. Except in this quite extreme case, legal responsibility for actions are attributed to the whole person and should be, as any person who cannot control the various selves can be a danger to society. But in purely personal matters, the view in this book implies less quick condemnation of actions that one doesn't like.

Many, more ordinary psychological disorders are exaggerations or extremes of the normal MOS routines. Part of the difference is this: everybody does crazy things sometimes, but normally the order in life returns. When it is difficult or impossible to return to the control of daily life, a person may need to seek help.

If there is a line between a normal reaction to difficulties and a disordered one, it is somewhat like the difference between a brief bout with the flu and a chronic illness. It is one thing to feel sad when a love affair ends, or to cry uncontrollably when a parent dies; it is another to be so disturbed that for three years you cannot go to a party. It is one thing to be anxious about going to a party and another to be so afraid of meeting people that you cannot go outside your house at all.

Sadness becomes depression, happiness becomes mania, fear becomes phobia, concern becomes paranoia. Some disorders are mild: they may interfere with work, mood, or relationships. Some are more extreme: they cause people to lose all contact with the world as it is normally experienced. Some people can be incapacitated by their condition; some are even dangerous to others or to themselves; some are just different.

The mental operating system works to maintain order in a chaotic world. We select a small amount of information, interpret and organize it into categories, and remember a small, meaningful bit of what happens. Disorders can occur when there is a malfunction, breakdown, or misapplication of one or more of these processes.

Suppose your hearing is failing and you do not know it. You may think that others are whispering in your presence. Normal perceptual processes interpret the sensory input in the simplest meaningful way: people are whispering because they do not want you to hear them. It may be that they do not like you or they may be conspiring against you or plan to exclude you from some activity. A condition known as sensory paranoia may result from this kind of interpretation of faulty information. Order and disorder are two sides of the same coin.

We are all influenced by the particular experiences of our life. We may grow up under extreme or unusual circumstances: being beaten by our father or never receiving affection from either parent. We may have a strange series of accidents that create an unusual view of the world: suppose everyone in the family was murdered or had terrible luck in business. We might take this unusual experience as representative, overgeneralize from it, and think and act very differently from the other people.

In everyone's life there are times of extreme stress, times when we are more vulnerable and less able to cope with the problems of living. Violence and riots occur more often during heat waves; there are more admissions to mental hospitals during times of economic hardship and recession. Many of the disorders are, of course, less extreme than multiple personalities, but they often indicate that a normally integrated single piece of the mind has gained undue dominance. Sometimes the normal balance of developmental factors is absent. Here is what happens when the feeling talents are missing.

Suppose you saw this advertisement:

Are you adventurous? Psychologists studying adventurous carefree people who've led exciting impulsive lives. If you're the kind of person who'd do almost anything for a dare and want to participate in a paid experiment, send name, address, phone number and short biography proving how interested you are.

This ad was written by a psychologist and appeared in several underground newspapers in Boston. It attracted a number of people who, psychological tests revealed, fit the clinical picture of an antisocial personality (also called a psychopath or sociopath). Here is one case that vividly illustrates what can happen when a part of the multimind is absent: the remainder of the person can develop abnormally.

The psychologist Elton McNeil described one such person whom he knew, not as a patient but as a friend. One day McNeil and Dan F. were at a restaurant. When their order arrived, Dan F. yelled at the waitress, telling her that it was not fit to eat and demanding that she taste the food. He asked for the manager. When a second plate of food was brought, he shoved it aside, saying that it could not be fit to eat, either. McNeil asked about the scene:

> "Dan," I said, "I have a sneaking suspicion that this whole scene came about just because you really weren't hungry."
>
> Dan laughed loudly in agreement and said, "What the hell, they'll be on their toes next time."
>
> "Was that the only reason for this display?" I asked.
>
> "No," he replied, "I wanted to show you how gutless the rest of the world is. If you shove a little they all jump. Next time I come in, they'll be all over me to make sure everything is exactly as I want it. That's the only way they can tell the difference between class and plain ordinary. When I travel I go first class."
>
> "Yes," I responded, "but how do they feel about you as a person—as a fellow human being?"
>
> "Who cares?" he laughed. "If they were on top they would do the same to me. The more you walk on them, the more they like it. It's like royalty in the old days. It makes them nervous if everyone is equal to everyone else. Watch. When we leave I'll put my arm around that waitress and ask her if she still loves me, pat her on the fanny, and she'll be ready to roll over any time I wiggle my little finger."

He was convincing. I believed him. That's exactly what he did on the way out and there was no mistaking the look in her eye. She was ready any time he was, and she thought he was a lot of man . . .

One night, a colleague of Dan's committed suicide. My phone started ringing early the next morning with the inevitable question "Why?" The executives at the station called but Dan F. never did. When I did talk to him, he did not mention the suicide. Later, when I brought it to his attention, all he could say was that it was "the way the ball bounces." At the station, however, he was the one who collected money for the deceased and presented it personally to the new widow. As Dan observed, she was really built and had possibilities.

Dan F. had been married twice before, a fact he had failed to communicate to his present wife, and as he described it, was still married only part time. He had established a reasonable basis for frequent nights out since his variety show required that he keep in touch with entertainers in town. He was currently involved sexually with girls ranging from the station manager's secretary (calculated) to the weather girl (incidental, based on a shared interest in Chinese food). The females of the "show biz" species seemed to dote on the high-handed treatment he accorded them. They regularly refused to believe he was "as bad as he pretended to be," and he was always surrounded by intense and glamorous women who needed to own him to feel complete as human beings.

Dan F. had charm plus. He always seemed to know when to say the right thing with exactly the proper degree of concern, seriousness, and understanding for the benighted victim of a harsh world. But, he was dead *inside*. People amused him and he watched them with the kind of interest most of us show when examining a tank of guppies. Once, on a whim, he called each of the burlesque theaters in town and left word with the burlesque queens that he was holding a party beginning at midnight with each of them as an honored guest. He indeed held the party, charging it to the station as a talent search, and spent the evening pouring liquor into the girls. By about 3 A.M. the hotel suite was a shambles, but he thought it was hilarious. He had invited the camera and floor crew from the television station and had carefully constructed a fictional identity for each: one was an independent film producer, another a casting director, a third an influential writer, and still another a talent agent. This giant hoax was easy to get away with since Dan had read correctly and with painful accuracy the not so secret dreams, ambitions, drives, and personal needs of these entertainers. What was staggering was the elaborateness of the cruel joke. He worked incessantly adding a touch here and a touch there to make it perfect. [Italics added.]

How did he get like this? In his own words, Dan F. well describes his condition and how it came about:

I can remember the first time in my life when I began to suspect I was a little different from most people. When I was in high school my best friend got leukemia and died and I went to his funeral. Everybody else was crying and feeling sorry for themselves and as they were praying to get him into heaven I suddenly realized that I wasn't feeling anything at all. He was a nice guy but what the hell. That night I thought about it some more and found out that I wouldn't miss my mother and father if they died and that I wasn't too nuts about my brothers and sisters, for that matter. I figured there wasn't anybody I really cared for but, then, I didn't need any of them anyway so I rolled over and went to sleep.

The antisocial personality seems to be associated with decreased feeling, especially to unpleasant stimuli: it reacts less to shock. Some of the tendency might be inherited.

Certainly no one inherits antisocial behavior, but what might be inherited is a deficient feeling talent, an autonomic nervous system that does not respond to external stimulation. In most people the autonomic nervous system controls emotional responses, such as responding with fear when we do something wrong, and activates our reaction to an emergency.

In the appropriate situation, missing such an important piece of mind could lead to some deficiencies in learning law-abiding behavior, to less responsiveness to others' feelings, and to the need to create excitement—all characteristic of the antisocial personality. The normal mental operating system rules go wild.

In most people, mental routines develop through feedback in the environment: when a child is punished or slapped for doing the wrong thing, the activated feelings of hurt and guilt make it less likely that the action will be repeated. People with "flat" emotions would not feel the hurt and would be less likely to learn law-abiding behavior.

One characteristic of these people is extreme calm, perhaps due to the underarousal. The normal feedback given to the MOS does not develop, perhaps due to a genetically transmitted lack of activity in the autonomic nervous system. These people are constantly searching for mental stimulation in different situations; they attack others verbally and set up wild scenes like the burlesque queen party.

Multiple and antisocial personalities are hardly the only evidence for multimind. They are highlighted here because they allow us to see the workings of the normal multiple controls and feedback systems when they are disturbed. There are reams of evidence from studies of brain damage in which a particular piece, such as verbal memory, tone recognition, or a component of personality, is destroyed. There is evidence from the chemical side as well. Drugs that interfere with one part of the complex neurotransmitter system, serotonin, dopamine, or norepinephrine, can have devastating effects on the mind. LSD can fit into and completely disrupt the serotonin system, while extremely encompassing mental states like mania can disappear almost completely with the administration of lithium.

Schizophrenics can find their mental worlds shattered; their thoughts careen from one portion of the mind to another. Possession states occur, as do fugues, in which whole eras of a person's life are lost. All of these are extremes of the simplifying pieces of the mind that usually manage to coexist inside our skull.

We have to learn to treat people with such disorders differently than we do. We have to learn that a problem in one part of the mind may well be treated by a specific remedy and that this treatment may have profound effects on the other "people" who live inside as well. All these personalities—multiple, dissociated, split, undeveloped— are evidence that residing within us are many different selves. This general view, of the warring nature of the person, has been for the most part the province of the Freudians and Jungians.

When I have spoken recently about the multimind idea, there is always a question about the psychoanalytic viewpoint. Isn't multimind the same? Not really. Freud brilliantly tried to connect these ideas of the day with the symptoms of the patients he saw in an heroic and far-reaching synthesis. This view postulates a kind of undertow flowing deep within the mind, an unknowable unconscious that can ultimately control our conscious actions. The person, to Freud, is like a horse and a rider. The horse most often controls where the person goes, but the rider can say, "I wanted to go there anyway." Further, the person is divided into id, ego, and superego, all separate functions of mind, each with differing priorities and each seemingly in perpetual war with one another—especially the conflict between our "old" animal self and the "new" conscious rational parts.

There is a seductive romance to reading Freud, a feeling that one is in the presence of a genius. But he had little developed scientific knowledge to work with, and the system he created has been for all real purposes sealed to substantial modification and development for too long. It has remained fossilized like many other nineteenth-century theories, although it has had much influence with literary intellectuals because of its breathtaking scope and brilliant writing.

From a viewpoint almost a hundred years later, it is clear that our situation is more complex than the one Freud described. We are both more and less in control of our destiny than psychoanalysis allows. We are not only the prisoners of our sexual and aggressive drives but of our particular assortment of small minds and more: of the chemicals in the food we have eaten, the position of the moon, the electrical charges in the air, the alcohol or drugs in our system, and even sunlight itself. There are much more profound differences between people than Freud thought—left- and right-handers, men and women, first and later born.

And what of all the famous Freudian slips and the important idea that much forgetting and lack of learning are determined by unconscious processes? It is here that the multimind and the psychoanalytic ideas are very different. I am sure that there is some motivated forgetting, especially in highly emotional instances: people may well repress memories of their father's sexual advances, and such repression may well have observable effects on those people. But there is no real evidence that these instances are common. I am sure that they are few and far between, and they probably do not happen to a person more than a very few times in a lifetime except in extreme cases, such as those that can result in multiple personalities. Freud and his followers probably exaggerated the extent of this kind of mental damage; it does not represent how the mind works but is a rare disorder.

Multimind is agreed that there are many varieties of retrieval of information in one mind at one time and that there is different access to knowledge in different parts of the mind. But these differences depend primarily upon the characteristics of the small mind that is operating when something is learned and when remembrance is tried. Sometimes a mistake is just that: the wrong schemata are engaged. Someone counting the copies coming off a duplicating machine may well count "six, seven, eight, nine, ten, *jack, queen, king*" without being accused of an unconscious wish to gamble while working. It is clearly a case of the wrong small mind swinging into operation at the wrong time, as when you may drive to your old home the first week after a move. It is not a wish to return, most likely, but simply the old patterns running as usual.

What might have been considered hypocritical behavior or examples of repression might well now be seen as a normal mental mechanism: *the small mind operating at any time may not have the appropriate memory in store or the behavior in its repertoire.* We may well be able to decide how to behave in a situation when we are calm and can see many ways of acting, but that does not mean that it can be done. The small minds that we think we may choose from may be unavailable to consciousness when we need them. We are determined by a much more complex system than Freud knew. And we may be able to override it in spots by learning to switch the small minds.

As Freud exaggerated by far the lower-level determinants of consciousness, he ignored the strong role of conscious processes in the mind. But we are also capable of much more conscious control of ourselves than this brilliant nineteenth-century thinker imagined: severe emotional or intellectual problems in infancy and in early childhood can be overcome if later experience compensates; severe traumas do go away if they are not subject to reinjury; people do get better without the kind of psychotherapy that he proposed.

Next to the single-minded view, psychoanalysis is perhaps the second most important Western theory of the mind, one that is often considered opposed to the Western intellectual tradition. This exclusive argument between the Freudians and the mainline psychologists has forced many people into different camps, opposing the small-minded rationalistic view with one centered on the sexual etiology of mental processes. But as the TWIT view is too simple, so is the Freudian. Much of the psychoanalytic theory posits that information is often ignored due to the subterranean control mechanisms: people intentionally ignore learning things painful to them, and so on. But the situation, in my view, is both more prevalent and less insurmountable. There are quite separate selves, with differing priorities, that move in and out of their own accord, sometimes under the governing self's control, sometimes on their own. The conscious control mechanisms are stronger than Freud originally thought, but they have a more difficult job.

The Western Analytic Tradition is too limited, and too

deterministic, focused strongly as it is on the sexual parts of the complex system of the multimind. But the psychoanalytic system does bring up the problem we have had: of devising a way to assess and understand others. We have been as poor at understanding others as we have been in understanding ourselves.

CHAPTER TEN

Knowing Oneself and Other Minds

WHEN WE ASSESS another person, we want a sample. We may speak to the person, invite him out to dinner if we are considering hiring him, or perhaps go to the ball game. We get to know each other by piling up the samples, piecing them together, and determining what they mean.

In making formal personality and intelligence assessments, professional psychologists do the same thing. However, in both personal life and formal testing it is often hard to know what is the correct sample and what is the correct inference from your information.

If you leave $10 on the desk and the prospective maid doesn't steal it, is she honest? If your boss works late into the night, is he conscientious at home as well? If your prospective son-in-law hates the Yankees, does that mean he should marry your daughter?

Remember the waiter who suggested that you try a slightly less expensive entrée? Is he trustworthy? No; this is a known strategy to get you to spend more later. The smart waiters, better psychologists in this matter than the professionals, learn to give you a small sample of apparently trustworthy behavior, knowing that you will generalize from it.

Scientists, psychologists, and educators have been no better than laymen in determining the correct way to assess others. A high tech modern technique, such as recording the microvolts of brain waves available on the scalp, gives no more real information about character than does reading the rate of toenail growth or tarot cards or a Rorschach test, but it seems more scientific.

Educators and students of the mind have always looked for the single, simple key that will give a complete assessment of others. For centuries, the accuracy of visual acuity, the force of a grip, the speed of auditory tracking, the growth rate and size of hair follicles, have all been analyzed, as have eye color, the speed of tapping, the degree to which a person is consistent in answering personal questions, and the ability to copy figures, to read paragraphs, to draw, to pay attention to several things at once, to extract the hidden figure from many, and to assemble blocks.

People have looked at muddy inkblots, had their EEGs read, had their heads measured, been asked questions about meaningless paragraphs, done mathematical calculations, given of their blood (blood typing and its relationship to success in business is a new fad in the Orient) — all in search of the key that will easily explain others. And the test results should reduce to one number, or at most two, so that we can fit it into a simple category in our MOS.

The same procedure of mind is at work here as the one we described before. It doesn't matter whether it is a first trip to Paris or a first date, a first encounter with Moroccan food, Australian films, or Dante. Due to our standard assessment procedure, a new person is considered most often in binary terms: is he or she more or less intelligent, aggressive or docile, conscientious or lazy, shallow or profound? Simple-minded first impressions are formed on the basis of snap judgments.

The consequences have sometimes been disastrous. Formal assessment has as its aim, for the most part, simple characterizations of people, characterizations that may well stick with the person for life. That someone is "educable mentally retarded" or exhibits "paranoid ideation" is fairly easy to conclude from an hour or so of testing in an isolated room, but at what cost to them for the rest of their lives? The same thing happens to individual lives as well, as we judge other people.

A divorce lawyer once said to me, "I've seen hundreds of divorces in my career. I can understand why people get divorced, but what I don't understand is when someone, after five, ten, or even *twenty* years of marriage, says, 'I never really knew him.' How is it that someone can live with someone else every day and never know them?" This problem occurs to the rest of us, too; we wonder how someone could just take off like that. "He had always seemed so conscientious." Or we can't understand what one person sees in another, or, for our purposes most revealing, we think, "She's not herself today."

In order to think that someone is not herself, we must have an idea of just what she really is. But this is where we get into the problem, because there is no real self in the way we usually understand it. Our idea of the self is just that, a constructed idea, an image in the mind of the beholder—and even in the beholdee.

It would be nice to be able to promise a clear and simple answer to the puzzling question of why our own selves and those of others are so difficult to know. To understand a whole personality, like understanding a person's intelligence, involves characterizing and assessing people. The same process of discovery has once again occurred in the scientific psychological community: a generalized and simple idea, followed by smaller ideas, leads finally to an understanding of the different and complicated components of the mind—and, thus, of the person.

The study of personalities has had a great popular history in psychology; Sigmund Freud has been judged by *Time* magazine as the most important figure of the twentieth century. There have been many famous and conflicting early visions of the person, such as those of Freud and his camp, including Jung, Adler, and Rank. There have been many different reactions to Freud, by Carl Rogers, Hans Eysenck, Abraham Maslow, and various behaviorists. Meaningful questions have been debated. Is our personality formed before the age of five? Are we in the grip of forces beyond our ken? Is our behavior determined by the contingencies of the situations or by our inherited predispositions. Is rationality possible to man? Are there transcendent faculties beyond the personal unconscious? Are we dominated by our unconscious? Is there an unconscious, anyway?

With a multiple view of the mind's faculties, we can put these questions into perspective, along with the warring views of Chomsky and Skinner, cognitive science versus ethology, rational man versus one who uses often mistaken and simplifying fast paths to judgment.

From the new evidence on the mind, the problem with the controversies many have read about is they are the result of a primitive and tentative understanding of the mind. They each focus upon one part of the multimind and claim that part as representative of the whole. Each viewpoint is expressed in absolute terms: we are capable of growth; each of us has a self that can encompass difficulty; we are determined by drives that cannot be controlled; we are the result of our environment acting upon us and there are no heroes, no freedom, no dignity. No matter how well developed or how popular, these questions that have preoccupied us are all early and simple-minded attempts at categorizing people.

The great discussions and endless arguments about which simple-minded system is better — psychoanalysis, behaviorism, humanistic psychology, and more — is the elephant-in-the-dark type of thinking. We assume the person must be wholly explainable as introvert or extrovert, in the dynamics of Freudian sexual hydraulics, in specific responses to the events of one's life, or in the potential for growth.

The familiar progression was from the grand designs of the person in the mold of the psychoanalytic model to smaller designs, then to a view here that considers the person as a complex mosaic of traits. The modern tradition began with Freud, whose ideas were derived in part from the discovery of the mechanism of evolution. The theory was startling, as he saw us doomed to live a life of conflict within society, the prisoners of our outmoded animal instincts of sex and aggression. Later theorists as well as Freud himself reacted to this completely bleak description by returning more pieces to the puzzle of personality.

Later adherents of psychoanalysis modified its viewpoint. Some felt that the ego or self was stronger and more capable than Freud did; some, like Jung, felt that we have access to a deeper pool of unconscious knowledge. Others believed that personality is primarily social or primarily one of self-development and self-actualization. Each view pretty much ignored the others in an attempt to promote a grand design. This grand and general personality approach, so similar to that of the search for general intelligence, a general and equipotential brain, and the general rules of learning, soon fell into general disuse.

After the breakdown of the Freudian synthesis, the next

step was the postulation of different general types of persons. A type is one with many consistent characteristics, such as those pointing to introversion or extroversion or the currently modish Type A. "Type" is a level of explanation that we feel comfortable with, as in "She's the very friendly type." But this simplification, too, is one of our illusions: the general type is just too general to hold up. People are not so consistent as to behave true to type. One person may be quite warm toward others at the office but may well be aloof in social relationships, another the reverse: which one is really the friendly type?

So the analysis went down one level to traits, which are units close to those of the talents and modules of the brain. One set of traits, developed from countless statistical studies by Raymond Cattell, includes brain-based talents such as "verbal fluency" and "affected by feelings" along with many other more general components, like "serious" and "conscientious." Probably these kinds of characterizations will be the next to go, since "conscientious," like "friendly," is in the eye of the beholder. But this view of Cattell and others is probably, in its general structure, close to the truth. It means that an individual cannot be assessed quickly and simply by the kinds of tests that have been done in the past. Each of us has a collection of diverse abilities, all of which make up our selves.

Part of the problem of understanding others lies in the particular structure of a person's talents, and part lies with the mental structure of the judge and the theorist—especially in the perceiver's tendency to make snap judgments, to overgeneralize, and to oversimplify.

People are certainly the most complex "objects" we ever perceive; they have different genetic predispositions, different histories, and they seem different depending on our needs, interactions, personality, and perception. When two women are discussing the same man, one may say, "He's so domineering," the other, "He's so sweet."

Because they have many separate and independent talents, different people seem to have a lot of identities within, and these change with different situations. Think back to Indiana Jones in *Raiders of the Lost Ark,* who was both a swashbuckling adventurer and a meek professor. None of us is simple.

There is an important scene in Lawrence Durrell's *The Alexandria Quartet,* a set of novels about a group of people in Alexandria, Egypt, and how they came to know one another. The books focus on a woman named Justine and how others see her. To one man, Justine is a selfish lover; to another, a committed revolutionary. We wonder, all through the books, who she *really* is.

But Durrell has anticipated some of the lessons of contemporary psychology. Near the end of *Justine,* he portrays a scene of her dressing before a mirror with several panels, like those in stores, in which we can see ourselves reflected from different angles. We show, he seems to say, different sides of ourselves, depending on the point of view of the onlooker and the situation. It is because these sides are really the different small minds swinging into operation in different situations that makes it so difficult to understand her.

This simplifying costs us more in the perception of other people than it does in the perception of the outside world. We use the same kind of prototypes in judging people as we do colors and brightness and chairs, but the mental structure just doesn't fit. We try so hard to make other people become perfectly coherent and stable, like our perception of genuinely stable objects like rocks and cups. We categorize or prototype individuals as, for instance, a hot-tempered redhead or a meek professor or the strong, silent type, and we are often surprised when people do not behave as they "should."

Many people have a surprising experience the first time they hear their voice on tape. The taped voice sounds high-pitched and squeakier than we think it is. "That's not me, I hope," is a common reaction. On tape, our voice is heard as we hear others, not with the bone and skull cavity vibrations that feed in to our own perception.

There are, as we noted earlier, different kinds of information available to the governing self portion of the mind about internal and external events. The information differs in amount and kind. We have a great amount of available information about ourselves, but it is not comprehensive; we don't really know how we sound, we don't know how we look from the side.

I have lost the hair on the top of my head over a period of fifteen years. For about ten of those years, I combed my hair from the sides over the top to cover it. When I looked at myself as I usually do in the mirror, the covering hair made me look like a man with a full head of hair. But as I began to notice other men in my situation, I could see them from other angles. It looked stupid: a thin stripe of hair was followed by the characteristic round patch of skin. Once I finally registered that I also looked like that, I first hoped that my haircut would become a new punk style. But it didn't, so I swept what was left straight back.

There are great differences in how we experience ourselves and how we experience others.

William James wrote:

> A man has as many social selves as there are individuals who recognize him and carry an image of him in their mind . . . he has as many different social selves as there are distinct groups of persons about whose opinions he

cares. He generally shows a different side of himself to each of these different groups ... We do not show ourselves to our children as to our club companions, to our masters and employers as to our intimate friends.

One man may regard himself as quiet and dependable at work but as fun-loving and carefree in social relationships. Many centuries ago, Plato had Socrates proclaim the aim of philosophy: "Know thyself." But the process is quite complicated, more so than we have ever believed.

It is unlikely that we were born with some kind of a real self that we can discover; rather, we construct our own idea of ourselves within from the different kinds of information available. This happens, probably, in the frontal lobes of the brain.

We also develop and learn about the self through observing our own internal states and behavior. Most of the time we know how we feel about something, especially when there are no conflicting conclusions within. We may know that we generally dislike a particular person or are excited or angry about a particular event.

But often there can be ambiguity: we have mixed feelings or the different centers of the brain come to different decisions. In such a case, there may be a discrepancy between how we expect to feel and how we actually feel, how we want to behave and how we do behave. Then the comparative processes go to work and a calculation is performed about our feelings, a calculation like those complex ones described earlier in considering cognitive dissonance.

In our everyday life, we are generally unaware of the conflicting interpretations and direct perceptions of our inner feelings, just as we are unaware of the organization and interpretation that guide our perception of the outside world. A parachutist who is about to jump out of a plane does not think, "My heart is beating rapidly, therefore I am afraid"; he or she simply feels afraid and is.

However, in very clever psychological experiments it is fairly easy to demonstrate that this sort of interpretation can occur. If you give some false feedback of the subject person's internal state, you can see how this information is automatically and unconsciously incorporated into his or her judgments and feelings.

In one experiment, a group of young men listened to the sounds of their heart while looking at slides of *Playboy*-type nudes. But there was a trick: the sounds that the men heard were artificial simulations of the heart rate. When some of the slides were shown, the apparent heart rate was speeded up. Of course, the men rated those photographs as the most attractive. Other experiments have shown that the same kind of false information (amplified heart rate) can make some people feel more afraid in a threatening situation. It is the wrong mind, here the activating talent, switching in and persisting.

Many seducers attempt to create such a hopeful confusion of increases in heart rate. They may try daring exploits, some deliberate arousing, or risk. Otherwise, why would horror movies, roller coasters, or driving absurdly fast be such common teenage pastimes on dates.

So we see ourselves in the same general way as we do others except that we have direct access to some parts of ourselves and are unable to observe other parts. We simplify everyone. MOS actions reduce the complexity of the outside world to standard items easy to act on.

A very important problem we face in understanding others and ourselves is consistency. We assume that a child whom we perceive as honest does not cheat at school or on the playground and does not steal from the corner store. But what would happen if you actually followed the child around for several days and kept a record of his or her actions?

In a classic study, the psychologists Hartshorne and May and their colleagues did just that. They studied more than 8,000 children and assessed their "moral character" by their behavior in a number of diverse circumstances—cheating in the classroom and on exams, stealing money, lying, and cheating during games—and found that there was very little consistency of behavior across situations. Rather, they found that a person's behavior is situation specific, in the trade jargon. Being honest or cheap or condescending or conscientious in one situation does not mean that a person will be the same in a different situation. This finding has been demonstrated repeatedly. So, perhaps the consistency we find in others is a function of our own small-mindedness: it may lie only in how we simplify our perceptions.

We have a kind of easy and automatic paranoia about other people which comes naturally to the MOS. We always try to make people simple and to perceive some of their personal characteristics as linked, using the same kind of prototypes we use to decide about birds and chickens. So, in most observations of other people, we are likely to see their behavior as consistent. But if we see them in other roles, the behavior may well change. Contrast, for example, how the police captain and his attorney girlfriend (and later wife) in the television show *Hill Street Blues* act toward each other at work, where their roles often force them into conflict, and off the job, where they are very close and loving.

We just cannot get beyond our limitations most of the time; we cannot perceive behavior as random or multiply determined. This is just too much for the MOS. Rather, we perceive it as coherent and meaningful. We try to make sense of others' actions and attribute the right reasons for their behavior.

What little information is available is overused: the more we know about someone, the less likely we are to do this. We also tend to attribute our own behavior to the situation and others' to dispositions. We are more likely to attribute our successes to internal dispositions (e.g., intelligence, skill) and our failures to the situations (e.g., bad luck or task difficulty). When Jimmy Carter won the presidency, it was reported that he attributed it to his own brilliance in organization, his skill in campaigning, and his motivation. When he lost, it was reported that he attributed it to the problems of the economy, the energy crisis, and the international situation.

There is a kind of built-in illusion of the self in judgment. We tend to overestimate our own contributions and our own role in affairs. In academia, two researchers who work on a paper may each believe that it is his or hers, and each thinks up strategies to get his or her name first. It has often seemed to me that alphabetical order for publication is often suggested by someone whose last name begins with a letter early in the alphabet.

Granted that these processes do exist, that we do tend to overgeneralize about others, still, our idea that we—both ourselves and others—are coherent and consistent still feels correct. Why are we so wrong and so deluded, and how are our judgments faulty?

We see that our boss is friendly to others as well as us, makes a special effort to help people with problems, and really seems to be generally a nice person. How do we form these impressions and how can we understand our limits of knowing others?

When we first meet a person, we rapidly form an

impression of his or her basic characteristics. This impression, or snap judgment, is based not only on the person's verbal and nonverbal behavior but on our past experience. For example, a man in a singles bar may be more likely to notice blond women if he usually dates blondes, and he is more likely to notice whether the woman is wearing a wedding ring if he meets her in a bar rather than at his job.

We possess only partial information about other people, yet somehow we form a coherent impression of them. Solomon Asch suggested that this is so because people's characteristics, or traits, form simplified and consistent patterns of impressions. For example, we are more likely to associate being industrious with being intelligent and skillful than with being frivolous.

We seem to assume, as did the personality theorists, that some traits are more central than others; they dominate the impression and organize it very differently. Asch gave subjects lists of traits and asked them to write a paragraph describing the characteristics of that person. Group A heard about a person described as intelligent, skillful, industrious, *warm,* practical, and cautious. Group B heard about a person described in nearly identical terms: intelligent, skillful, industrious, *cold,* determined, practical, and cautious. The two groups formed quite different impressions of the person; clearly, if we think a person is warm, we are likely to infer specifically different characteristics than if we think he or she is cold. Somehow certain traits seem to go better with others. It is simple-mindedness at its most destructive and stupid.

Some of the effects of such simple-mindedness are quite weird. A man comes in to give a lecture to students. Afterward, the students are told that he is either a student or a professor and are asked to rate the lecture. Not surprisingly, they rate the lecture as being better if a professor has given it, but what is surprising is that they rate the lecturer as *taller* if he was identified as a professor. A big man, indeed! A fast path, the similarity routine, seems to have these unintended consequences. Tall men also get more pay, more sexual advances; sexy women get worse pay (it can easily be changed by dress!); redheads are thought to be hot-headed (probably because of the color association to fire), bald people are thought to be intelligent (probably because of the amount of head visible), thick-lipped people are thought to be continuously sexy (probably because the lips temporarily swell during arousal).

How do we see each other, then, as stable? Why? One clue is that most people's self-descriptions are remarkably stable across time, even over a number of years or decades. Perhaps being consistent in different situations is not the same thing as being consistent over time. In studies of conscientiousness, people were found to be very consistent over time in the same situations but not consistent in different situations.

So we probably are the ultimate in simple-mindedness about others. We select only a few items about each person to go into the fast path judgments, as we do for everything else. We try to make them more stable than they are. We may quickly judge someone, for instance, as a prototypical kindly old man and then try to fit his actions into the "correct" category. Or, more likely, we select a few key features that go along with being, for instance, kindly and restrict our observation to them, largely *in the same situation*, over time. Because behavior *is* consistent in the same situation over time, we can maintain our coherent perception ("He is honest"; "She is conscientious") and simply ignore many other situations and behaviors of that person.

So we *impose* a consistency on other people. It is a complicated process that the multimind goes through in order to misinterpret people: we take these partial observations in specific situations and fill in the gaps, creating our vision of other people. This is why people are actually less consistent than they seem to us. Perhaps consistency, in addition to beauty, lies in the eye of the beholder.

We have tried the same oversimplified routines in assessing intelligence, too. Those who do not exhibit what we consider intellectual abilities are discarded, and the rich array of artistic, intuitive personal skills are discarded, and discarded too quickly, in favor of a bean-counter mentality. It is unfair and unwarranted, but it is no joke. We must do something about the way we test and assess people.

The multimind idea may help avoid many tragic mistakes in testing people. With a more complex understanding of the mind, we may well be able to assess a person's many talents that we often overlook in producing a simple viewpoint. And we may get a new view of the different selves within ourselves.

Because the ideas behind the study of intelligence have been so undeveloped and simplistic and have had such a great influence on us, it may be useful to look at how we came to have "the quotient" and how it came to have such undue influence on our life.

IQ is an abbreviation for "intelligence quotient," and it is thought by many to be a genuine and almost physical component of a person, like height. People are sorted by IQ into different streams of education and different lives, all on the basis of a paper and pencil test that lasts a few hours at most.

It seems so simple: anyone understands that to be intelligent is to use the mind well. But on examination we may mean very different things by this statement. Someone may be thought smart for working out an elegant proof in mathematics and also for producing a striking painting. There are brilliant chess moves, football plays, and stock buys.

Most people and many psychologists think that intelligence is a single, fixed quantity: someone is either smart in almost all things or not. From the analysis presented here, this viewpoint is clearly wrong. Intelligence is rather a limited judgment we make of others based on their array of talents. The common element is that someone acts with excellence and originality in (what is considered by those judging) the best way.

But different societies have quite different concepts of intelligence. The West, ever since the philosophical Greek myths described earlier, is the heir to a tradition that values verbal and rational thinking above all else. In a formal assessment of other minds, it is here that our simple-minded view has cost us so much. Someone who thinks logically and communicates effectively is obviously thought intelligent in our society. We would be more likely to call a lawyer intelligent than a riverboat guide. But there are societies in which the mark of an intelligent person is one who can guide a boat down a river well. It is by no means clear that the same person would be judged intelligent in both societies. Would the boatman be able to guide a jury? And how well would our lawyers handle boating skills? We judge people intelligent because of their possession or development of a few of the many talents of mind.

The early work sought a simple and single intelligence, a standard against which many other minds could be measured. The history shows, for the most part, how difficult it has been to decide what intelligence is and to apply it to individuals. Until quite recently, it has been difficult to come up with anything more useful than the simple-minded approaches.

Traditionally, only the rich could afford to educate their children. Then, in the late nineteenth century, universal public education became compulsory. Suddenly, teachers did not know how to teach all these children from different backgrounds and with different degrees of preparation for school. The testing that was necessary was to have a profound and unexpected effect on our ideas of intelligence.

In 1904, the French government asked Alfred Binet to devise a test that would predict which children would be most and least likely to succeed in school. To meet society's demands, intelligence testing would have to be able to sort large numbers of children into "bright," "average," and "below average" ranks. The French schools used the results of these tests to assign children to classes; below average children were either given special training or excused from attendance. Binet had created a helpful test that suggested how these masses of children should be distinguished in schools.

Would that Binet's influence had stopped there. And would that it had been developed into a more complex and more profound set of complete tests of the mind.

A few years later, another profound event directly affected intelligence testing: World War I broke out. This war was vastly different from any waged before in many ways, but for our purposes it was the first war in which millions of men from the general population were required to fight. In the United States, the army needed to know the capability of its unknown, untrained, and untried soldiers.

The specific scores became more important than they had been in Binet's original tests, because they were the primary factor in determining the soldiers' assignments. But the wartime necessity of group administration of tests and the rather strong reliance on the test score as the primary measure of a person's intelligence remained the norm even after the war ended. And it has continued.

A great deal of research has been done in the effort to find a single and general intelligence. Charles Spearman tried to measure this G, an entity that in the quaint neurophysiological language of the day related to something called cerebral energy — and some of the currently uninformed of our day are still trying to do the same thing, using measures such as the brain-evoked potential.

Spearman assumed that a single general intelligence would characterize each individual. However, we have too many separate talents to yield a single number. Individuals are as different in the nature of the separate small minds of the MOS as they are in their memory, perceptions, and their ability to learn.

Each individual in the normal range might better be considered as made up of a variety of abilities, not more or less generally intelligent than any other. One person may perform well on verbal tasks while another may be good at fitting objects together and a third may write well. When children are given several different tests of mental ability, some excel on some measures, others on different ones.

These and other findings have led psychologists to move a step toward multimind and to consider that there are many different abilities that make up intelligence. As more research findings come in, the picture keeps getting more complex as more different abilities are added to the puzzle, one after the other, from one intelligence to two to one hundred and twenty. Smaller and smaller pieces of mind.

I think there is a far superior, if less neat, way to describe it. The important component lacking is the wheeling and dealing aspect of intelligence, the unpredictible participation of the many small minds. Just because we have one ability does not mean that we will use it in the proper circumstance. This is the kind of mental development that should be taught to teachers.

Each person's intelligence is best considered a mosaic of specific intellectual abilities and talents that form an individual portrait of intelligence. One person may be good at art and bad at math, another the reverse, a third good or bad at both. One "smart" person picks the right stock; another "smart" one proposes a new theory. Intelligence is a judgment based on many separate abilities. People are much more individual in their assortment of characteristics than we normally give them credit for.

There are people with good memories for faces and others who are good with names; there are people who are good at finding their way in new surroundings but can't hear music or reason; there are those who can reason but can't find their way around. There are musical abilities that are separate from those intelligences that Howard Gardner calls the personal. I am often reminded of a comment, "You may know a lot about psychology, but you sure don't know anything about people!," which sums up much of the academic approaches, for the most part.

And people probably differ in the way in which they use their talents: some people seem able to keep six wheels spinning at once while others attend more deeply to one thing at a time. Cultures have radically different approaches to the training and the cultivation of the mind, and when these differences arrive at simple-minded testing sites, lives are ruined.

The assessment of children based on the single IQ score has caused more destruction and pain than any other product of our simple-minded approach.

IQ tests are used to classify children in schools, and those who score low, between 60 and 70, for example, may be placed, as they are in California, into classes of "educable mentally retarded" (EMR), where the scholastic program is much less challenging than that for children with higher IQs. Sometimes this division is warranted and humane. There are some severely retarded or disturbed children who could not keep up in a traditional public school. Most of the time, the standard tests do discriminate against children whose backgrounds differ from the norm. A child who answers the question "Which goes with a cup?" with "a table" (choosing from a chair, a saucer, and a table) is marked as incorrect on a certain test (that is now obsolete). But if the child was too poor to have saucers, he or she would see the cup on the table. Is that child less intelligent? How much of this business of differences in intelligence is due to matters of race and background and how much due to genes?

The largest controversy has been about the concepts of race and IQ. Both are simplifying prototypes that exist only in the perceiver's mind, and it is no surprise that there is such controversy about whether people of different races inherit different IQs.

It is very difficult to measure precisely the exact relationship between heritability and IQ. Estimates vary greatly:

one is that 81 percent of IQ is inherited, another gives the much lower figure of 25 percent. Most investigators agree that there is some heritability of IQ, although whether it is great or small is quite difficult to assess. Indeed, it would be surprising if there were no genetic component to IQ. The information encoded in the genes could fill approximately 1,700 book pages. Some of that information might be related to the reasoning and problem-solving skills that are important in human evolution and that are tested by the IQ.

But the question of race and IQ is explosive. As early as 1916, Lewis Terman of Stanford, who developed the Stanford-Binet test for use in the United States, noted that "high grade moronity" was "very common among Spanish, Indian, and Mexican families . . . and was among Negroes." But this is a problem in large part of the simple-minded view of the perceiver. Race is a meaningless concept, more of a perceived trait than anything that makes sense biologically.

People evolved different skin colors to adapt to different climates. In fact, there are any number of ways to categorize and classify human beings into races: by height, hair color, eye color, nose size, and others. A person's skin color tells you nothing more about intelligence than hair color. The major differences between races are skin deep: they consist of superficial adaptations such as skin color, eye folds, and sweat glands. There is no evidence of differences in brain size, shape, organization, or structure or in any other mentally relevant classification, although there are quite strong differences between individuals.

People get their genes from their parents, not from a group. However, even if race were a more profound and real distinction between different groups of human beings, the evidence is scanty regarding any differences in intelligence between "black" and "white" genes. Consider the results of interracial marriages, where the genes for intelligence should be equal: however, the IQs are not equal. Children of a black father and a white mother tend to have higher IQs than children of a white father and a black mother. White women talk to their children more than black mothers do. This also gives us a major clue: the home environment, especially the mother-child relationship, may have an important relationship to IQ.

Race is not the only prototype of the mind; IQ is also. The IQ is not intelligence, not a mental talent, but a test score developed by Terman from Binet's test and designed to distinguish between children who could and who could not profit from normal schooling. The idea, as we have seen, is scientifically obsolete, anyway. The human intellect is a composite of different abilities, and there is no single number that can adequately indicate a complex human intelligence.

It is almost idiotic to conclude that blacks are genetically inferior in intelligence to whites or, as some now do, that whites are similarly inferior to the Asian students who are doing so well in schools in the United States.

It would be much more profitable for all concerned if we focused our attention and effort on developing tests that might identify the specific talents of the child and on enriching the environment of children who suffer deprivations.

If we do have a diverse array of talents within, then there might well be more hope for many people abandoned by the single-minded approach of our educational system. There will be more benefit to society as well. With a different, less categorical emphasis, many of those lacking verbal and logical talents may be able to improve their education and develop their own intelligence.

In the past few years, many programs have strengthened the notion that the components of intelligence can be developed. Most of the factors that seem to affect the IQ differences between whites and blacks in the United States are experiences in the environment. But it can be changed: improved nutrition and more stimulating environments have systematically increased IQ scores. Preschools and Head Start programs in the United States and an ambitious program in Israel are currently attempting to increase the IQs of disadvantaged children whose IQs are far below normal.

Orphanages can have a negative effect on a child's mind, because they are often bleak places that offer little human contact and minimal external stimulation. In Dennis's study in a Lebanese orphanage, the average IQ of the orphans was 63; in a well-baby clinic, 101. When these orphans were simply propped up in their cribs for an hour a day so that they could see what was going on, they showed dramatic improvement.

Howard Skeels decided to find out whether stimulation and attention (tender loving care) are important in the development of intelligence. He placed 13 orphans with an average IQ of 64 (with a range from 35 to 85) in an institution for retarded adults, and each orphan was "adopted" by an older woman. All the adoptees became favorites of and were doted on by the patients and staff. A control group was selected, comprising children between 1½ and 6 years old, who remained in the same or a similar orphanage. The control group's IQ dropped an average of 20 points. The "adopted" orphans gained an average of 28 points.

The results of Skeels and others encouraged the development of various enrichment programs aimed at increasing IQ. Many parents now send their children to preschools in the hope that such early training will enhance intellectual development. Children in preschools typically show an initial increase in IQ and a decline to the norm at around the second grade.

The programs that emphasize academic skills alone are most likely to show a later decline, while those preschools that emphasize curiosity and self-motivation, such as Montessori schools, show the greatest long-term gains. Among the most successful interventions to improve mental talents, at least in the United States, are those that attempt to change the pattern of mother-child interaction.

These programs are successful probably because many skills important in schooling depend on language for expression, and language skills develop within the family. The mother spends much more time with her child than do teachers and has been the primary language teacher (at least before the era of television). Changing the mother-child interaction seems to be an important intervention in increasing intelligence.

There are other, more innovative programs that seek to develop intelligence. In one new intelligence test, the student learns something during the test rather than recalls information. The assessments are longer, and the tester spends much more time with the student and observes him learning new skills. These tests of such adaptability or cognitive modifiability hold much promise, and many countries are attempting to use these new measures to develop the mental talents of their citizens.

So intelligence is really just one of our general ways to describe others, and scientists have been taken in by their own mental illusions. With a multiple idea of the mental diversity within and the diversity of the components of our personality, there might be some progress now in the understanding, educating, and taming of a few of the multiminds. Otherwise the tragedy of wasted lives will continue, due to our simple-minded view of ourselves and others.

PART V

THE GOVERNANCE OF THE MIND

After a long journey, Nasrudin found himself amid the milling throng in Baghdad. This was the biggest place he had ever seen, and the people pouring through the streets confused him.

"I wonder how people manage to keep track of themselves, who they are, in a place like this," he mused.

Then he thought, "I must remember myself well, otherwise I might lose myself."

He rushed to a caravanserai. A wag was sitting on his bed, next to the one which Nasrudin was allotted. Nasrudin thought he would have a siesta, but he had a problem: how to find himself again when he woke up.

He confided in his neighbour.

"Simple," said the joker. "Here is an inflated bladder. Tie it around your leg and go to sleep. When you wake up, look for the man with the balloon, and that will be you."

"Excellent idea," said Nasrudin.

A couple of hours later, the Mulla awoke. He looked for the bladder and found it tied to the leg of the wag. "Yes, that is me," he thought. Then in a frenzy of fear he started pummelling the other man: "Wake up! Something has happened, as I thought it would! Your idea was no good!"

The man woke up and asked him what the trouble was. Nasrudin pointed to the bladder. "I can tell by the bladder that you are *me*. But if you are *me* — who, for the love of goodness, AM I?"

— Idries Shah, *The Subtleties of the Inimitable Mulla Nasrudin*

CHAPTER ELEVEN

Who's Minding the Store?

"HAVE YOU changed your mind?"

There seems to be an apparent conflict in the minds of many people about how one person could write from apparently divergent viewpoints. I wrote earlier, in *The Psychology of Consciousness* and in *The Mind Field*, about the unexpected possibilities of the development of consciousness. But later, in *The Amazing Brain* and in this book, I make the strong claim that the brain is an incoherent, bizarre, and ramshackle device and that we have great difficulty in controlling our minds.

"How can you say that we unconsciously wheel in these separate small minds and also are capable of 'an extended understanding of the meaning of life'? Are we really able to go beyond the customary norms of thinking, or are we forever just prisoners of our limited system of mind?"

"*Which* is it?" I have been asked more than once. It is not, I hope, that I am becoming less coherent and precise in my middle age. It is just that my constant object of inquiry, the human mind, has come more clearly into view. There have been tremendous advances in the study of human evolution, neuroscience, cognitive science, which now allow a broad sketch of the incoherent, complex, and dissonant nature of the complete mind.

It never seemed that there was a problem in describing the potential of mind in the development of consciousness as well as the limits of mind in the way we usually act like automata. They are both part of the human mental system, although many people will admit to neither. In fact, many of the writings in the traditional psychologies strongly emphasize the continuously automatic or inflexible nature of human knowledge. We are capable of great understanding and are also oblivious to important information, making misjudgments and mistakes.

Many questions stem from either-or kinds of thinking. The multimind idea explains (or, perhaps, describes) why we have so many conflicting thoughts about ourselves, about the nature of specific people in our lives, and about human nature itself.

Why can't I control myself?

Do I love him or hate him?

Is she a good person or not?

Are human beings beasts or angels?

Is it possible for people to go beyond the normal understanding of self?

Obviously these are not either-or questions, even though we try to understand ourselves this way. I hope this book helps to dispel the oversimplified views we have of ourselves. There are diverse, divergent, and multiple minds, and the contradictions come with the territory of being human. We are a more extraordinary animal than we think, but also a more dangerous one; we are closer to destruction and to transcendence than we know, in a race with the different pieces of our selves.

In writing this book, I have not tried to pile case upon case or to list exhaustively all the studies currently available or all the evidence necessary for making a complete case for the multimind, although many may have found quite enough details as it stands. Others may still find the view incomplete. What about the learned component of our abilities, such as the very great cultural differences and those of languages? Where do they fit? There are many other abilities and portions of the mind that do not seem to be covered, such as creativity, suspicion, temperament. Obviously I have not presented a complete account of how everything happens in the mind, merely a new perspective. I don't think our knowledge is advanced enough to present a complete account, nor will it be for a long time.

My aim is much more general. There is a new understanding of the mind and a new psychology in the making, and I hope to press the current perspective outward. You will note that I have taken only two of the many possible main lines for my argument. The first is from the classic studies of the research tradition of modern psychology. The second comes from Madison Avenue, where ideas have quite definable consequences: the bottom line.

There is much more information and entire research traditions that bear on the argument that we are not unitary or consistent. For instance, the results of subliminal stimulation studies provide intriguing evidence that parts of our minds are quite permeable to subtle influences.

There is also new evidence, quite radical in its implications, that comes from many studies by Kenneth Ring and others, who have observed people who have clinically died and been revived. Ring and others have collected reports that when a person dies, she or he still has a form of consciousness. I won't follow up this line except to note that this evidence, if well documented, would take the argument far beyond that advanced here.

A natural question arises: Where in all this is the "me"

who is responsible for our actions? This question has not had much attention in psychology since the time of William James. Part of the problem is that psychologists and educators have forgotten entirely the ideas of will and volition. Yet it is this component of the governing self that links many of the separate small minds. The view that there are any number of semi-independent small minds, each designed for a purpose, space, music, time, emotions, expressions, thinking, social roles of the mother, the daughter, the lover, the employee, also brings up the question of who runs the show.

In part, the "me" who is responsible and whom society recognizes as responsible resides in the ability to control the diverse systems within. Something has to command the wheeling in and out of one or the other small minds. But this is a controversial point, since many cognitive and philosophically minded psychologists feel there is nothing left for the mind to do once we have enunciated many of the components or modules of the mind, the very many separate abilities described in this and other books. In this view, the separate minds clamor and fight for control and the strongest wins, with no directing force. Some feel the question of control is only a pseudo question. Others believe that it is unnecessary for psychology to assume a self on aesthetic grounds, as it seems an unnecessary element. They feel it is preferable to make the simplest (called the most parsimonious) assumptions about the mind, for this to the academic is supposed to be the Way All Science Progresses.

This piece of the TWIT mentality again tries to make the mind neat and analyzable, in conformity with one of the most basic principles of the multimind's action. Simplified explanations, to ordinary perceivers and to scientists, always seem preferable. It usually works that way in the simpler sciences like physics, where it is usually a matter of defining the single nature of an entity, even a subatomic one. Psychologists have often thought they could become "real" scientists by emulating the physicist's methods.

The problem is that the mind is not a simple system, and its physiological underpinnings evolved in an almost impossibly complicated way. Consider color vision, whose nature inspired earlier versions of the single simple mechanism argument: certain phenomena, such as the three kinds of color blindness, argued for a three-process theory. Other phenomena, such as the red-green and blue-yellow reversals in afterimages, provided opponents with the argument that color is a two-process operation. Which it was was argued for decades.

It was both: there are receptors for three kinds of color information in the eye, and the signals are sent to the brain in two processes. It is not parsimonious, not neat, but we didn't do the designing. So, in the vastly more complex area of mental functioning, these simple-minded approaches won't do. I am sure that the already complex view of multimind will be replaced with an even more complex understanding in the future.

Another challenge that is made especially to me is this: "You have written more than most about the Eastern esoteric psychologies. In all these, the self is often ignored as part of human understanding. Does this not show that there is no need to assume the existence of a self?" In my view, those psychologies are constantly denying the self as a means of getting it out of the way.

For it is just the normal egocentric means of understanding, probably mediated by the governing talents, that prevent people from going beyond self-centeredness. The techniques for avoiding pride — the ideas that "*I* shall progress, *I* know," and so on — are attempts to get rid of this talent as an exclusive means of understanding so that other faculties can come forth. And it is most common to almost all traditions of human development to recommend self-observation as a primary method, if not knowing oneself, at least observing oneself.

El-Arabi ("Dr. Maximus"), who died in the thirteenth century, wrote: "The Sufi abandons the three 'I's. He does not say 'for me,' 'with me' or 'my property.' " There are countless examples in Christian, Buddhist, Muslim, and other traditions of forced deprivation of the ordinary desires for companionship, food, sleep, recognition, and much more. These are self-extinction procedures; all were originally intended to break the normal control of the governing self over much of the rest of the mind.

In some especially prescient traditions, this part of the mind is even called the commanding self. I highly recommend Idries Shah's *A Perfumed Scorpion* for an extensive discussion of the many selves in man. This extraordinary book contains an analysis of the possibility of self-understanding far beyond that of this book. It is an "advanced" psychology. To take just one example, many of the stories of the Sufi tradition contain descriptions of the interchanges between pieces of the mind. These pieces are symbolized as different characters. Here is one, from Shah's *The Magic Monastery,* about the control of a person's actions:

Where It Starts

A certain Sufi master was walking along a country road with one of his disciples. The disciple said:

"I know that the best day of my life was when I decided to seek you out, and when I discovered that through your Presence I would find myself."

The Sufi said:

"Decision, whether for support or opposition, is a thing which you do not know until you know it. You do not know it through thinking that you know it."

The disciple said:

"Your meaning is obscure to me, and your statement is dark, and your intention is veiled from me."

The master said:

"You will in a few moments see something about the value of decision, and who it is that makes decisions."

Presently they came to a meadow, where a farm worker was throwing a stick to a dog. The Sufi said:

"I will count five, and he will throw three sticks to the dog."

Sure enough, when the Sufi had so counted, the man picked up three sticks and threw them to the dog, even though they were out of earshot and the man had not seen the pair.

Now the Sufi said:

"I will count three, and the man will sit down."

As soon as he had counted to three, the man did indeed sit down, suddenly, on the ground.

Now the disciple, full of wonder, said:

"Could he be induced to raise his arms into the air?"

The Sufi nodded and, as they watched, the man's hands rose towards the sky.

The disciple was amazed, but the Sufi said:

"Let us now approach this man and speak with him."

When they had saluted the farm worker, the Sufi said to him:

"Why did you throw three sticks instead of one for the dog to retrieve?"

The farm man answered:

"I decided to do it as a test, to see whether he could follow more than one stick."

"So it was your own decision?" "Yes," said the man, "nobody told me to do it."

"And," said the Sufi, "why did you sit down so suddenly?"

"Because I thought I would rest."

"Did anyone suggest it?"

"There is nobody here to suggest it."

"And when you raised your arms in the air, why was that?"

"Because I decided that it was lazy to sit on the ground, and I felt that raising my arms towards the Heavens would indicate that I should work rather than rest, and that inspiration to overcome laziness came from on high."

"Was that a decision of your own and nobody else's?"

"There was, indeed, nobody to make such a decision for me, and in any case it followed from my previous action."

The Sufi now turned to the disciple and said:

"Immediately before this experience, you were saying to me that you were glad you had made certain decisions, such as the one that you should seek me out."

The disciple was completely silent. But the farm worker said:

"I know you dervishes. You are trying to impress this hapless youth with your powers, but it is sure to be a form of trickery."

Concerning the self from the viewpoint of more formal psychology, it is clear that many components of the understanding of oneself can be destroyed by brain injury, especially to the frontal lobes. Many more psychological phenomena, like those of cognitive dissonance (the tendency to compare our thoughts within our own mind and achieve some consistency), would not occur unless there were an entity in the mind to make the necessary compromises. I don't think it is as well articulated as Billy Milligan's Arthur, but I think something like that is present in the normal mind.

It is a separate mind that in most instances has to determine where the whole person stands on some issues, taking as evidence the diverse cognitions and behaviors. In some cases, this mind may well be able to override the various small minds that are trying to take charge and wheel in the correct response.

This means that something inside ourselves, some "one," must often calculate or infer our own thoughts and feelings as a result of a continued observation of our behaviors. In one sense, this is the most important contribution of the research on cognitive dissonance and the rest of the cognitive tradition: we can only calculate and infer our own opinions as the result of an odd kind of observation of ourselves.

I remember being startled once during a casual conversation with a writer for the local newspaper. I asked him about the private opinions of a well-known columnist on his paper, and he quite surprised me when he said, "All I know about him is what I read in the newspaper." I think a similar process goes on inside the multimind: all our separate minds know about each other is what they observe to be happening. They do not have the intimate access one would assume, as I had assumed about people who work for the same newspaper.

We constantly observe ourselves this way. When we are coming down with a fever, we often first experience a mild internal upset, which may be misunderstood: we might attribute it to disagreements with one's spouse, difficulty at work, and a host of other possible explanations until we realize we are sweating and feeling alternate chills and cold and accept that we are becoming physically ill.

The process is similar to a child's self-observation of what is happening internally. A young child may fly into rages, become upset, or get depressed until he or she knows, by enough repetition, that he or she is tired or hungry.

Deficiencies in nutrition or unexplained illnesses can completely swamp our consciousness with thoughts of "What's wrong?" until the real cause of the depression is discovered: "Oh, I'm sick!"

It happened to me once in a situation that was like the false feedback experiments described earlier. I am normally a blithe lecturer, as I give only one lecture during any year, usually based upon my current research, so I am quite prepared. One day I flew down to Los Angeles to give a lecture and sat on the podium awaiting my turn. I started to get nervous, shaky. I was worried about my presentation. "Why didn't you prepare more, why didn't you bring more slides?" and more went on inside. I was worked up and nervous. Then I looked down at my hand. It was trembling, shaking; I couldn't even hold a glass of water. I didn't know what to do. Should I just leave before I gave an embarrassingly bad lecture?

Then I looked again at my shaky hand, and I noticed that the microphone on the stage was shaking. Then I saw that the floor was shaking, all over the podium.

It was the air conditioner, which had started up as I reached the podium, and its compressor pulleys were vibrating the whole room and vibrating me. But I didn't know that, and the part of me that wished to explain what was happening interpreted this shaking as internal, the result of nervousness about the lecture. Once I saw the air conditioner, I was no longer nervous; I knew the real cause of my discomfort. And my intense self-observation was satisfied.

However, this kind of thinking can go too far: we obviously have another set of minds that for the most part respond quickly to the world. We know red when we see it. We know something that makes us angry. We know when we are pleased. We are a mixture of this direct perception of the world and our assumptions, guesses, and calculations.

We can be an object to ourselves and we have to know what is happening to us. Philip Zimbardo has pointed out that different people have their own characteristic explanations when something goes wrong: "It must be something I ate"; "It must be something someone did to me"; "It must be something I did"; "It must be something in the room"; "It is our———political system that denies me rights." To make this kind of judgment, we may have to reconcile many of the incoherent messages in our own mind. I am sure that the observer part of the multimind does just this, but the situation is probably more complex than the view taken by social psychologists. We probably strive for a consistency of cognitions, but we probably need to do this within many of the separate multiminds.

The observation mind is probably a dormant faculty in most people, because there is usually little reason to notice that there are different minds taking control at any time. It is a part of the mind that probably can be developed by first observing the alternations, gradations, and changes that "come over" us, then noting that it is not always necessary to accept the multimind that is "automatically" called up in a situation — say, your child yelling at you, your habitual emergency response to a deadline, and so on.

It is a question of who is running the show. In most people, at most times, the automatic system of the MOS organizes which small mind gets wheeled in, most likely on that automatic basis of blind habit. But there is a point when a person can become conscious of the multiminds and begin to run *them* rather than hopelessly watch anger wheel in once again.

Are we automata, controlled by genes, by our inheritance, by the environment, or by some combination? Is it all "God's will," no matter what? I think a consideration of these questions using the multimind concept will be more useful than previous approaches. If there is any will, it would reside in the selection mechanism of the separate minds that get called into play. If there is an automaton in us, it is in the thoughtless selection of the mental routines that get called up: Do we have to get angry about an injustice? Is it useful to judge things through the window of comparison or can we change the frame?

On looking at the mind this way, it seems likely why there is so much confusion about free will; obviously some people have more than others, and some "mental development" routines can increase the ability to select the small mind that is to operate. From this viewpoint free will exists, but it is a small and weak force in most minds, a force that probably can be developed by self-observation, a look at how one is acting and at the relationship between the situations one finds oneself in and the actions that ensue.

It does seem, on the basis of the experiences of many who have practiced it, that such self-observation gets the potential for change into the controlling areas of the mental operating system, just as whenever a problem needs action it comes into consciousness. Through this kind of self-observation we come to know the divergence that is our multimind and our responses become more stable: when the antics of the MOS can be observed in one's own mind, it seems that awareness leads to a lessening of the reflex selection of small minds that enter consciousness; "Oh, yes, it's time for the emergency routine again."

People can learn to observe the automatic selection of a small mind and observe which factor — external, food, personal, social, environmental — is really causing a given reaction. Once we know what is bothering us we are able to change somewhat, just as I was no longer bothered by the shakiness once I realized that it was the room and not I.

Under the stimulus of self-observation, the MOS seems to begin to change and the fixed links between action and reaction are loosened, leaving room for some serious choices and redirection of the mind.

It is here that the religious and philosophical methods of mental development cast some unexpected light on our conceptions of mind, for the ideas of "man" being "fallen," "blind," "asleep," or an automaton are all consistent with the view that we are also capable of mental development beyond the norm but usually are the prisoners of the automatic selection routines of the MOS.

Increasing self-observation and less self-centeredness are part of normal psychological development. The Swiss student of development Jean Piaget described decentration, the process wherein our initial and quite extreme egocentrism declines as we age. It is a process like that of our scientific understanding. Before Copernicus we believed we were the center of the universe; before Darwin we believed we were special creatures; before Freud we believed we were the masters of the mind. Piaget felt that the same thing happens in early life.

During the first stages of life, the newborn often cannot tell what are his thoughts and what is outside him, even whether there are any other people in the world. The viewpoint is, "The world is I." Thus lights, flashes, internal rumblings of the mother, are all the same. Later, small children decenter, become aware of the existence of other people and objects, both animate and inanimate, but remain quite egocentric. They are unable to imagine the world from any viewpoint than their own: "The world is as I see it."

As children begin to reason (around the ages of 5–8), they make a further step, in Piaget's view; they recognize that there *are* other ways of looking at the world. However, they generally think theirs is the only correct way: "I have the right view of the world." In adolescence a new ability of the self emerges, the ability to imagine and idealize things. Then the child characteristically believes that the idealized view is preferable for all: "The world *should* be as I see it." This view often persists and becomes part of the different views we have of ourself and others. Some people criticize politicians for taking stances they feel are inconsistent; others criticize writers for not doing things their way; and many more suffer from this "terminal assistant's disease." It can be found in any company or organization. With increasing life success, these kinds of unfortunate reactions cease, but not always.

While Piaget is probably too categorical and rigid in his analysis, I am sure his general outline of the process is correct; there is less extreme egocentrism as we age. But of course we are still left with the normal self-centered adult. Using the process of self-observation, we may be able to realize that our own view of the world isn't even singular and constant, that we have many different and conflicting views inside us all the time. The process of self-observation may convince some part of us (I don't know which) to give voice to alternate views and actions.

The tennis star Billie Jean King said after entering her thirty-fifth Wimbledon tournament; "When you're young, you think you're the center of the universe. When you're older, you realize that you're just a little speck." This progression is not unlike the understanding in these supposedly alien esoteric traditions.

And a similar comment might be made about how we know and treat other people in our lives. They embody many different and conflicting views as well. The assumption that other people can be simply and easily understood, that they have fixed intelligences, and that they are consistent, whether good or bad, causes much trouble. And if there is one lesson to be learned from the study of the multiple minds and the selves within, it is that other people are more complex than we might be able to perceive.

So, the next time someone you respect does something you don't like, you don't have to change your assessment too quickly. If you say, "I think he is kind," and find that the person does something that you don't consider kind, remember that there may be many reasons for it. You may not have enough information. He may not consider the action unkind. He may be inconsistent; there may be other parts of his personality operating.

You may not like some parts, perhaps entire "subpersonalities," of someone, but there is a problem: people come in large and inconsistent packages, like other groups, teams, companies, and the like. These people may swing in different small minds at times, some of which you may find objectionable. The problem is for the judge of others not to be too swayed by small pieces of another's mind. The man who has gone through several wives, quoted at the beginning of the book, has never understood that one can only accept people as whole entities and as they are, for people do act very differently toward other people at different times and in different situations.

If someone is inconsiderate in one situation, perhaps there is a reason you don't know about. If someone is not conscientious at work, perhaps they understand their job differently than you do. If someone has an annoying reaction to stress, it does not have to be the end. Either you learn to live with it or simply avoid getting caught in that kind of trap. Saying to yourself: 'Here swings in that small mind again; it'll be gone soon," might be a help sometimes in waiting things out.

Considering others in the same way we consider groups or crowds, like our company, favorite team, or restaurant, might be the shift in understanding we need to make. "I like the food, but not the decor," neatly separates different functions, and we can decide whether to go to the restaurant again. The same approach could be used in marriage and in other close relationships. We are not consistent: one part of us may say something and mean it but become overwhelmed by another small mind. This does not mean that we are untruthful but that a different part has become active.

Inconsistency is part of the package of being a complex human being, and we should not try to imagine otherwise. I think Westerners have an automatic idea that when someone says something, they are speaking the truth—"I give you my word," and so on. But obviously we place much too much emphasis upon a person's exact words. The talking talent does not really speak for the whole person. If we understood this more deeply, we might avoid the kinds of conflicts that can destroy otherwise useful relations. Many times we may think that something is a deliberate lie when it is just the talking talent saying what is on its small mind at the time. Many arguments are misinterpretations of one small mind saying its piece and then going away. And many uttered "truths" are really perishable; they are true for a while, and then something else comes along.

We do not know ourselves or each other. Our view of others is partial, oversimplified. We use simplifying strategies like their traits and race and categorize them. We pass each other like ships in the night; we send out a small and partial signal to each other, and we receive it with a part of our minds. We are not able to know others completely in all their complexity.

And our own selves are hidden from us as well.

But, then, how *do* we develop and change, given the multimind view? It is an important question, because we are at the beginning of a new understanding of ourselves which brings up new possibilities.

It is in the ability to select the reaction, to select the mind that is operating, that is real mental development, not the blunting of the personal faculties in meditation or relaxation, although in other cultures meditation has been one means of preparation for a new kind of self-control. There is a lot of confusion about the nature of mental or conscious development, as many seek to change their minds by forgetting their abilities — by meditating, eating only vegetables, losing their reasoning and critical abilities — and this gives other, more active, people a distorted idea of the process and the possibility of conscious change.

Conscious development probably consists of attaining a genuine measure of understanding and control of the wheeling and dealing mental system: being able to choose which of the small minds (if any) operates at any moment. Perhaps the most important implication of the multimind metaphor is that people may be able to recognize that they and others may have a great many different talents and abilities. With their development, many people may well be more able to respond to life as it really is, not as we would reduce it to fit one small-minded view.

We must be able to learn and train ourselves in how we think, how our minds are structured, and how we can overcome the innate limitations and biases of mind. We are far beyond ourselves now and parts of us must catch up.

There is a mental system, comprising many diverse, even warring small minds, that seeks to keep things simple and consistent, and it has brilliantly evolved a few major strategies to guide us through conditions that were appropriate for our ancestors. But these simple strategies, and our self-deception that we are whole, stable, rational thinkers, are often at the root of many personal, social, and political problems. It is the judgmental part of the multimind that particularly needs to catch up. It is quite unfortunate that we have to judge everything using these almost automatic policies of mind, but I hope that elucidating the many mechanisms and the many different distortions and results will make us face our multiple minds and our limited mechanisms of judgment. Perhaps we will start to become conscious of our limitations and begin to change.

I said at the beginning that this book is an attempt to push toward a new perspective, from which many new developments might emerge. Our understanding of the nature of the mind is, I believe, the current barrier to solving many problems that are now seen to have only political or administrative solutions. We are a more dangerous animal than we would like to think, but we can change more than we might have dreamt by calling on and calling out some of the very many diverse mental abilities within ourselves. The first step is in understanding the multiple nature of our mind.

NOTES AND COMMENTS
REFERENCES

16 Descartes' quotation is from his massive and classical work *Meditation on First Philosophy,* translated by L. J. LaFleur (New York: New York Library on Liberal Arts/Liberal Arts Press, 1951; original publication, 1861).

I neither wish to overemphasize Descartes' achievements nor to decry the mind-body dualism that is synonymous with him. Descartes did send the modern era into motion with his discussion of how the signals from the conscious mind get into the body. For the most part, his influence has not been that constructive, as it insinuates that these are in principle different entities. The multimind idea may allow us to realize that there are many different minds, some of which control the body, some of which do not.

For this discussion, I wish merely to highlight Descartes as one of many possible thinkers (Spinoza and Kant also come to mind) whose work has been central in framing our viewpoint on the mind, the brain, and cognition.

20 As an example of the current approach, Herbert Simon, a Nobel prizewinner in economics, has been recently quoted as saying that the aim of current computer simulation is "just trying to simulate a deep thinker sitting in an armchair—ignoring sensory and motor output."

This, to my mind, is one of the primary mistakes we are making in attempting to model the mind on a machine. It is the separation of the "thought" from the "sensory and motor" components of mind that seems to be the crux of much of the current difficulty. It's my viewpoint and that of an increasing number of investigators that higher conscious functions are not at all that separate from the sensory and motor routines that underlie them and that carry them out. Indeed, many of these "lower"-order phenomena consistently override directed thinking.

So, in order to get a better picture of the nature of the mind, the priorities should be very different: we should know much more about the biological responsibility of the mind and the different influences on it before attempting to simulate a paraplegic professor. Once we have absorbed the multiple nature of the mind, we might well try to simulate some of its activities, but it will take a generation of computers far beyond those currently being used. Perhaps 7,500 Cray3s would do, hooked up to do many different tasks. Modeling the mind on a computer will be much more like modeling the world economy or the world's weather three months from now than on anything like a paralyzed professor.

21   TWIT embodies a certain component of mind, the component that is unaffected by body states, that does not bear the consequences of decisions, the component unconcerned with sensory motor, personal movement activities. It is this "pure thinking" component that has been so prized. I think that in isolation this component will very much live up to the rather jocular acronym I have given it. If it were integrated as one of the many small minds that people possess, it would not seem so separate.

24   One of the newest approaches to intelligence by Robert Sternberg (in *Beyond IQ,* Cambridge: Cambridge University Press, 1985) tries to divide intelligence into three factors: problem solving, effective experience, and practical intelligence. The third part is what he calls tacit knowledge, the stored idea we have about the world. But this attempt, although better organized toward daily activity than the old IQ, still ignores the vast amount of activity

that the mind must process to go through the number of different reactions that go in and out of consciousness. I shall have more to say about this in Chapter 9.

27 Please see Jacqueline Ludell, *Sensation* (New York: W. H. Freeman, 1978), for a full analysis of the sensory processes.

28 I have reviewed the general overarching components of human nature in my own textbook, *Psychology: The Study of Human Experience* (San Diego: Harcourt Brace Jovanovich, 1985).

31 The quotation from Jalaudin Rumi comes from Idries Shah's collection, *The Way of the Sufi*. Rumi in many ways anticipated a number of the conclusions of contemporary science, including evolution and the shifting nature of our own personal judgments.

34 For a general treatment of the evolution of the brain, with superb illustrations by David Macaulay, please see *The Amazing Brain*, by Robert Ornstein, Richard Thompson, and David Macaulay (Boston: Houghton Mifflin, 1984).

44 I am using the word "module" in the dictionary sense. The operative definition of module, according to *The Oxford English Dictionary* (small print edition; page 1829), is "a regularly formulated plan or scheme," that is to say, a fixed or planned activity. Thus, the proper definition of module would also include analytical and output systems of the brain and, in an even more fixed manner, reflexes and other activities.

51 I don't think it is possible to overestimate the blunting effect of the Nazi atrocities and other brutal political events, including those in the United States and in South Africa, on our idea of our own nature and our own mind. Even someone who raises the idea that certain aspects of human personality and cognition may be genetically influenced is often vilified unmercifully. There seems to be a kind of barrier to arational consideration of these kinds of questions.

53 This discovery of the operation of the two hemispheres of the brain is recorded in my *The Psychology of Consciousness*, 3rd ed. (New York: Penguin Books, 1986).

54 There are a lot of ways to divide the mind's activities. Some of them, like Sternberg's *Beyond IQ*, try to do it in

terms of practical intelligences. Others, like Howard Gardner in *Frames of Mind,* do it in major categories of intellectual activity, like music and logic and mathematics. Gardner is more broad in his definition than most, as he includes personal factors in intelligence as well as movement factors. But I think the best thing to do is to begin our description of the mind using fairly straightforward brain-based activities and assume that the more complicated aspects of mental life are involved in their multiple participation.

I am aware that analysis is hopelessly incomplete and I am sure it will be challenged in certain ways, but I also believe it is a useful place to start. In any case, I assume that these will be superseded at a later time. It is, however, the wheeling nature of the mind that I believe to be most central to the multimind idea, not the specific nature of the separate components of the mind.

62   These quotations are derived from Howard Gardner's *The Shattered Mind,* which is extremely useful reading on the different components of mind that can be teased out by a careful and thoughtful analysis of brain-damaged individuals. It is an important book, and I highly recommend it.

76   The traditional organization of psychology, in which there are faculties like perception, learning, motivations, and so on, is what is called in the trade a "horizontal" analysis, in which we look at the perception of smells, forms, speech — everything — through the window of "perceiving." The different analysis that has come to be called vertical emphasizes that it is the faculty that is important, not the process.

Thus, smell has its own complete, "encapsulated" system, whether we are talking about perceiving, experiencing, sensing, or remembering it. And language has its own system, whether we are talking about hearing it, producing it, or trying to understand it. This idea probably makes much more sense in regard to how the brain evolved since it did not change as it developed, it simply added new and different components. It is undoubtedly true that the mechanisms that decode speech are entirely separate and even developed in different eras from the mechanisms that decode smell.

72 Some people may quibble with my use of the word "module" to cover a "prepared reaction," such as food or poison avoidance. But I hold that the idea of module being a fixed plan of action that is independent of the circumstances surrounding it is adequate. I believe that modular actions, reactions, and reflexes are a very important part of our makeup in an area that has not really been researched much.

76 I believe the phrenological reference is really quite apt. Franz Gall postulated the number of important faculties of mind and in so doing was very close to the modern analysis.

79 Here Nasrudin quite perfectly swings in the habitual small mind. He cannot at this point override his normal quick and immediate reaction. He thus demonstrates why consciousness is not always that important in our normal analysis of the mind. It is because the lower centers take precedence, and conscious control in most people at most times is very weak.

81 Much of the analysis identifying the "fast paths" of the mind has been done by Amos Tversky and Danny Kahneman, to whom I am indebted.

87 The most influential and most useful social psychological theory on which I am drawing is Leon Festinger's theory of social comparison. The famous work on this is his *A Theory of Cognitive Dissonance* (Stanford: Stanford University Press, 1957).

92 I am indebted as I am for much of the treatment of how many different factors influence our decisions to the remarkable book by Robert Cialdini called *Influence* (Indianapolis: Scott, Foresman, 1984).

98 The late Stanley Milgram probably contributed the most brilliant series of studies to social psychology. This is from his *Obedience to Authority* (New York: Harper & Row, 1972).

100 But it's also true in Asch's experiments that when someone is present who doesn't conform, people feel free not to conform to the large-scale judgment as well. Apparently, we don't need many people, either, to help us break

conformity. I wish psychology would study more of these "heroes."

104   The same arguments could be made with the other policies of mind as well. "What have you done for me lately?" forces us to an extreme, short-term sensitivity to recent phenomena. Our sensitivity to change information makes it important that we ignore almost all of what happens to us. See, for good examples: A. Tversky and D. Kahneman, 1981, The framing of decisions and the psychology of choice, *Science* 211:453–458; and R. E. Nisbett and L. Ross, 1981, *Human inference: Strategies and shortcomings of social judgment* (Englewood Cliffs, N.J.: Prentice-Hall).

107   I suppose the crux of many of the questions about consciousness concern whether *we* are really conscious or what consciousness is capable of. I think the framework here presents a way for people to understand that consciousness can be important but that it is not always important. In most cases, the small minds seemed to wheel in automatically and take control. It is only on rare occasions that people are able to consciously control the nature of their mind. This, I believe, is what "conscious development" is about. And this more complex view of consciousness will reconcile the viewpoint I took in *The Psychology of Consciousness* with other, more conventional, theorists who believe that consciousness is not very important.

134   It's hard to tell conclusively, of course, whether Milligan was completely genuine, although it would be difficult to believe that all of his "selves" were made up. However, Martin Orne has recently exposed a similar case in which there was a fraudulent use of multiplicity to avoid the responsibility of murder.

149   I believe it may be possible at some point in the future to put together all the separate factors—such as the weather; whether people are left-handed, first born, or later born; and the particular distribution of their talents — into a more reasonable computer analysis and modeling of the mind if we know about the particular selection processes of consciousness and the particular strengths of individual small minds. I believe some interesting work is under way with this general viewpoint directed by Professor Minsky

of MIT. He believes, along with many of us, that the mind is really composed of a number of separate information-processing systems.

165   Again, many of the newer approaches to intelligence testing fail here. They seem to wish to add only a few elements to the traditional approach. Sternberg's *Beyond IQ*, which was discussed earlier, merely adds practical and world knowledge to intelligence. It is no more intelligent than the IQ. It is perhaps a better predictor of school and vocational success, but again has very little to do with the mind, although it may be a more useful test.

Gardner's approach is probably more reasonable. *Frames of Mind* is quite close to the multimind approach, except that in that book he rather rigidly sets out certain spheres of intelligence and does not really discuss how they interact, how things come into consciousness, and how the higher and lower parts of the mind operate.

188   I believe many of the questions about the nature of consciousness — how it operates and whether the position I am taking here is different — will have been answered by now. They are answered by the understanding that consciousness is in fact not a very strong force in the mind. And while one can write, as I just said, glowingly of consciousness developing, this doesn't happen very often; it exists more as a possibility for some people than anything that is actually realized.

192   There are many stories in Sufi literature published by Idries Shah that allow a person to become more aware of the wheeling antics of the mind and the different selves that exist. Mulla Nasrudin's are perhaps the best examples, but there are of course many others. I particularly recommend *The Magic Monastery* for the story quoted here as well as *A Perfumed Scorpion* for a subtle and far-reaching analysis of the different selves. But any of Shah's books will serve as a useful introduction.

Here is a multiminded selection of readings. These books are highly recommended.

The Amazing Brain, by Robert Ornstein, Richard Thompson, and David Macaulay (Boston: Houghton Mifflin, 1984). It presents, especially in drawings, details of how the brain was constructed, the different centers of activity, and the way in which the different levels of the brain operate, from the cellular to the self.

Frames of Mind, by Howard Gardner (New York: Basic Books, 1983). An extremely well written and elegant review of a number of different parts of multiple intelligence.

Influence, by Robert Cialdini (Indianapolis: Scott, Foresman, 1984; paperback text edition). Excellent social psychology, it traces the many factors that influence decisions. It was a great, well, influence on me as I wrote this book. I have quoted heavily from it, but you should read the book on its own.

The Minds of Billy Milligan (New York: Bantam Books, 1983). An astonishing account of a case of multiple personality. While some aspects are very difficult to believe, it still presents in a coherent way some of the most interesting parts of human personality below the surface.

A Perfumed Scorpion, by Idries Shah (New York: Harper & Row, 1982). *The Exploits of the Incomparable Mulla Nasrudin* and *The Subtleties of the Inimitable Mulla Nasrudin* (London: Octagon Press, 1985). By our current premier exponent of how the different "selves" and minds work. They contain a fairly advanced form of story and discussion for people who are interested in observing the antics of their own mind and understanding how human consciousness, cognition, and development can progress. They are highly recommended.

All these books can be obtained from the ISHK Book Service, P.O. Box 1062, Cambridge, Massachusetts 02238. ISHK, a nonprofit institute of which I am the president, is devoted to making available to the general public work of enduring value and interest in the human sciences.

REFERENCES

Asch, S. E. 1946. Forming impressions of personality. *Journal of Abnormal and Social Psychology* 41:258–290.

———. 1951. Effects of group pressure upon the modification and distortion of judgments. In *Groups, leadership, and men,* edited by H. Guetzkow. Pittsburgh: Carnegie Press. Pp. 177–190.

Bennett, W. 1984. *Set point regulation of body weight* (tape). ISHK Book Service, P.O. Box 1062, Cambridge, Massachusetts 02238.

Bennett, W., and J. Gurin. 1982. *Dieter's dilemma: Eating less and weighing more.* New York: Basic Books.

Block, J. 1981. Some enduring and consequential structures of personality. In *Further explorations in personality,* edited by A. I. Rabin, J. Aronoff, A. M. Barclay, and R. A. Zucker. New York: Wiley-Interscience.

Brickman, P. 1975. Adaptation level determinants of satisfaction with equal and unequal outcome distributions in skill and chance situations. *Journal of Personality and Social Psychology* 32:191–198.

Bruner, J. S. 1978. Learning the mother tongue. *Human Nature* 1:52–59.

Cantor, N., and W. Mischel. 1979. Prototypes in person perception. In *Advances in social experimental psychology: Vol. 12,* edited by L. Berkowitz. New York: Academic Press.

Cialdini, Robert. 1984. *Influence*. Indianapolis: Scott, Foresman.

Cotman, C., and J. McGaugh. 1980. *Behavioral neuroscience*. New York: Academic Press.

Descartes, René. 1861; 1951 ed. *Meditation on first philosophy*. Translated by L. J. LaFleur. New York: New York Library on Liberal Arts/Liberal Arts Press.

Ekman, P. 1984. Expression and the nature of emotion. In *Approaches to emotion*, edited by K. Scherer and P. Ekman. Hillsdale, N.J.: Erlbaum.

Estes, W. K. 1980. Is human memory obsolete? *American Scientist* 68:62–69.

Festinger, L. 1954. A theory of social comparison processes. *Human Relations* 7:117–140.

———. 1957. *A theory of cognitive dissonance*. Stanford: Stanford University Press.

Festinger, L., and J. M. Carlsmith. 1959. Cognitive consequences of forced compliance. *Journal of Abnormal and Social Psychology* 58:203–211.

Feuerstein, R. 1979. *The dynamic assessment of retarded performers*. Baltimore: University Park Press.

———. 1980. *Instrumental enrichment*. Baltimore: University Park Press.

Feuerstein, R., and Y. Rand. 1977. *Studies in cognitive modifiability. Instrumental enrichment: Redevelopment of cognitive functions of retarded early adolescents*. Jerusalem: Hadassah-Wizo-Canada Research Institute.

Fodor, Jerry. 1983. *The modularity of mind*, Cambridge, Mass.: MIT/Bradford Press.

Freud, S. 1900; 1955 ed. *The interpretation of dreams*. London: Hogarth Press.

———. 1920. *Beyond the pleasure principle*. Standard edition, Vol. 18. London: Hogarth Press.

———. 1962. *New introductory lectures on psychoanalysis*. London: Hogarth Press.

Fromm, E. 1941. *Escape from freedom*. New York: Holt, Rinehart & Winston.

Garcia, J., and R. Koelling. 1966. Relation of cue to consequence in avoidance learning. *Psychonomic Science* 4:123–124.

Gardner, Howard. 1983. *Frames of mind*. New York: Basic Books.

———. 1985. *The mind's new science*, New York: Basic Books.

Gazzaniga, Michael. 1985. *The social brain*, New York: Basic Books.

Grice, H. P. 1967. Utterer's meaning, sentence-meaning and word-meaning. *Foundations of Language* 4:225–242.

Hartshorne, H., and M. A. May. 1928. *Studies in the nature of character: Studies in deceit.* New York: Macmillan.

———. 1929. *Studies in the nature of character: Studies in self-control.* New York: Macmillan.

Herrmann, D. J., and U. Neisser. 1978. An inventory of everyday memory experiences. In *Practical aspects of memory,* edited by M. M. Gruneberg, P. E. Morris, and R. N. Sykes. New York: Academic Press.

Herrnstein, R. J. 1973. *IQ in the meritocracy.* Boston: Little, Brown.

Herron, J. 1980. *Neuropsychology of left-handers.* New York: Academic Press.

Hinton, J. 1967. *Dying.* Baltimore: Penguin Books.

Hudson, W. 1960. Pictorial depth perception in sub-cultural groups in Africa. *Journal of Social Psychology* 52:183–208.

Humphrey, N. K. 1978. The origins of human intelligence. *Human Nature* 1 (12):42–49.

Ittleson, H. 1952. The constancies in perceptual theory. In *Human behavior from the transactional point of view,* edited by F. R. Kilpatrick. Hanover, N.H.: Institute for Associated Research.

Liebert, R. M., and R. A. Baron. 1972. Some immediate effects of televised violence on children's behavior. *Developmental Psychology* 6:469–478.

Locke, J. 1670; 1964 ed. *An essay concerning human understanding.* New York: Meridian.

Loftus, E. F. 1978. Shifting human color memory. *Memory and Cognition* 5:696–699.

Loftus, E. F. and J. C. Palmer. 1974. Reconstruction of automobile destruction: An example of the interaction between language and memory. *Journal of Verbal Learning and Verbal Behavior* 13:585–589.

Loftus, G. R., and E. F. Loftus. 1974. The influence of one memory retrieval on a subsequent memory retrieval. *Memory and Cognition* 3:467–471.

Lynch, J. 1977. *The broken heart: The medical consequences of loneliness.* New York: Basic Books.

Maccoby, E. E., and C. N. Jacklin. 1974. *The psychology of sex differences.* Stanford: Stanford University Press.

Maslow, A. H. 1971. *The farther reaches of human nature.* 2nd ed. New York: Viking Press.

Mischel, W., and P. K. Peake. 1982. Beyond déja vu in the search for cross-situational consistency. *Psychological Review* 89:730–755.

Myers, D. G., and H. Lamm. 1976. The group polarization phenomenon. *Psychological Bulletin* 83:602–627.

Nisbett, R. E., and L. Ross. 1981. *Human inference: Strategies and shortcomings of social judgment.* Englewood Cliffs, N.J.: Prentice-Hall.

Ring, K. 1980. *Life at death: A scientific investigation of the near-death experience.* New York: Coward-McCann.

Rosch, E. 1973. Natural categories. *Cognitive Psychology* 4:328–350.

Ross, L., D. Greene, and P. House. 1977. The false consensus phenomenon: An attributional bias in self-perception and social perception processes. *Journal of Experimental Social Psychology* 13:279–301.

Scarr, S. 1981. *Race, social class, and individual differences in IQ.* Hillsdale, N.J.: Erlbaum.

Scarr, S., and R. A. Weinberg. 1978. Attitudes, interests, and IQ. *Human Nature* 1 (4):29–37.

Seligman, M. E. P. 1975. *Helplessness: On depression, development and death.* San Francisco: W. H. Freeman.

Singer, J. L., and D. G. Singer. 1981. *Television, imagination and aggression.* Hillsdale, N.J.: Erlbaum.

Skeels, H. M. 1966. Adult status of children with contrasting early life experience. *Monographs of the Society for Research in Child Development* 31 (3):1–65.

Tennov, D. 1979. *Love and limerence.* New York: Stein & Day.

Tversky, A., and D. Kahneman. 1973. Availability: A heuristic for judging frequency and possibility. *Cognitive Psychology* 5:207–232.

———. 1981. The framing of decisions and the psychology of choice. *Science* 211:453–458.

Zimbardo, P. G. 1972. The tactics and ethics of persuasion. In *Attitudes, conflict and social change,* edited by B. T. King and E. McGinniss. New York: Academic Press.

———. 1973. The psychological power and pathology of imprisonment. *Catalog of Selected Documents in Psychology,* 30:45.

ABOUT THE AUTHOR

Robert Ornstein is president of the Institute for the Study of Human Knowledge. He teaches at the University of California Medical Center in San Francisco and at Stanford University and has done extensive research on the human brain. Ornstein is the author of *The Psychology of Consciousness* and coauthor of *New World, New Mind.*